D1709198

PIT BOSS Wood Pellet Grill and Smoker Cookbook

1800 Days of Outdoor Cooking Magic, BBQ Recipes, and Meat Masterpieces – Your Ultimate Guide to Irresistible Grilling Perfection!

Slistair Havenscroft

Table of Contents

INTRODUCTION

History and Features of The Pit Boss Grill And Smoker

Pit Boss Grills and Smokers have rapidly gained popularity in the barbecue and grilling community, known for their quality construction, innovative features, and affordability. The company behind these products, Dansons Inc., was founded by Dan Thiessen in 1999. Originally, Dansons started as a small welding shop in Alberta, Canada, but it soon transitioned into a leading manufacturer of wood pellet grills.

The introduction of Pit Boss Grills to the market marked a significant shift in the world of outdoor cooking. Traditionally, grills and smokers were fueled by charcoal or gas, but Pit Boss embraced the efficiency and flavor of wood pellets. This choice was a game-changer, as it combined the convenience of gas grills with the rich, smoky flavor associated with traditional charcoal and wood-fired cooking.

Key Features of Pit Boss Grills and Smokers:

- Versatile Cooking Options:

  One of the standout features of Pit Boss Grills is their versatility. These grills can smoke, bake, roast, sear, and barbecue, offering a wide range of cooking options. The ability to achieve various cooking styles makes Pit Boss a favorite among both beginners and seasoned barbecue enthusiasts.

- Wood Pellet Technology:

  Pit Boss Grills use wood pellets as fuel, providing a distinct smoky flavor to the food. The pellets are made from compressed hardwood sawdust, and users can choose from a variety of wood flavors like hickory, mesquite, apple, and cherry. The wood pellet technology also allows for precise temperature control, ensuring consistent and even cooking.

- Temperature Control and Settings:

Precision cooking is a hallmark of Pit Boss Grills. Most models come equipped with a digital control panel that allows users to set and monitor the cooking temperature with ease. This level of control is crucial, especially for long smoking sessions or when cooking delicate dishes that require precise temperature management.

- Generous Cooking Area:

Pit Boss Grills are designed with ample cooking space to accommodate large cuts of meat or multiple items simultaneously. This is especially beneficial for those who enjoy hosting outdoor gatherings or cooking for a large family.

- Durable Construction:

The build quality of Pit Boss Grills is notable. They are often constructed using heavy-duty steel, ensuring durability and longevity. The robust construction not only contributes to the grills' longevity but also helps in retaining heat, enhancing their overall performance.

- Innovative Designs:

  Pit Boss continually introduces innovative designs and features to enhance the grilling experience. This includes features such as a slide-plate flame broiler for direct flame grilling, removable racks for easy cleaning, and unique barrel shapes for optimal heat circulation.

- Affordability:

  Compared to some other high-end pellet grills on the market, Pit Boss Grills offer an attractive balance between quality and affordability. This accessibility has contributed to their widespread adoption among various demographics of barbecue enthusiasts.

In summary, the history and features of Pit Boss Grills and Smokers reflect a commitment to innovation, versatility, and quality. The incorporation of wood pellet technology, coupled with a focus on user-friendly features and durability, has positioned Pit Boss as a prominent player in the outdoor cooking industry. As the brand continues to evolve, it remains a favorite choice for those seeking a reliable and flavorful grilling experience.

Basics of Smoking

Smoking on Pit Boss Grills is an art that combines the rich flavors of wood smoke with the precision of modern grilling technology. Whether you're a seasoned pitmaster or a beginner, understanding the basics of smoking is essential to achieving mouthwatering results. Let's delve into the fundamentals that will elevate your smoking game on Pit Boss Grills.

- Choosing the Right Wood:

  The foundation of successful smoking lies in selecting the right wood for your Pit Boss Grill. Different woods impart distinct flavors to your meat. Common options include hickory, mesquite, apple, cherry, and pecan. Experimenting with wood combinations allows you to customize the taste of your smoked dishes.

- Temperature Control:

  Maintaining a consistent temperature is crucial in smoking. Pit Boss Grills, equipped with advanced temperature control features, make this process more manageable. For low and slow smoking, aim for a temperature range between 225°F and 275°F. This slow-cooking method allows the meat to absorb the smoky flavors, resulting in tender and flavorful dishes.

- Prepping the Meat:

  Before placing your meat on the Pit Boss Grill, proper preparation is key. Trim excess fat, apply a dry rub or marinade for flavor, and allow the meat to come to room temperature. This ensures even cooking and enhances the absorption of smoke.

- Setting Up the Grill:

  Understanding your Pit Boss Grill's layout is essential. If using a pellet

grill, load the hopper with high-quality pellets corresponding to the desired flavor profile. For offset smokers, arrange charcoal or wood on one side and place a water pan on the other to maintain moisture and stabilize the temperature.

- Smoke Production:

  To achieve the perfect smoky flavor, focus on consistent smoke production. Adjust the vent settings on your Pit Boss Grill to control airflow, preventing the fire from smoldering or flaring up. A thin, blue smoke is ideal for imparting a delicate smokiness to your meat.

- Monitoring Internal Temperature:

  Investing in a reliable meat thermometer is crucial for smoking success. Monitor the internal temperature of your meat, aiming for specific temperatures based on the type of meat being smoked. This ensures food safety and prevents overcooking or undercooking.

- The Art of Patience:

  Smoking is a slow and patient cooking method. Resist the temptation to frequently check or open the grill, as this can disrupt the cooking process. Trust the Pit Boss Grill to do its job and allow the magic of low and slow smoking to unfold.

- Enhancing Flavor with Mop Sauces and Spritzing:

  To add an extra layer of flavor and moisture to your smoked meat, consider using mop sauces or spritzing. These flavorful liquids can be applied during the smoking process, enhancing the taste and appearance of the final product.

- Resting Period:

  Once the meat reaches its target internal temperature, resist the urge to dig in immediately. Allow the meat to rest for a sufficient period, usually around 15-30 minutes, to let the juices redistribute. This step ensures a juicy and succulent result.

Mastering the basics of smoking on Pit Boss Grills opens up a world of culinary possibilities. From selecting the right wood to controlling temperature and adding personal touches with rubs and sauces, each step contributes to the creation of mouthwatering, smoky masterpieces. As you embark on your smoking journey, remember that practice, patience, and a willingness to experiment will ultimately lead to barbecue perfection.

Pellet Grill Tips for Beginners

Pellet grills have gained immense popularity among barbecue enthusiasts for their convenience, versatility, and ability to impart a unique smoky flavor to various dishes. If you're new to the world of pellet grilling with a Pit Boss grill, here are some essential tips to ensure a successful and enjoyable grilling experience.

Understanding Your Pellet Grill

Before diving into the cooking process, it's crucial to familiarize yourself with the basic components of your Pit Boss pellet grill. These grills consist of a hopper, auger, fire pot, and cooking chamber. The hopper stores wood pellets, and the auger transports them to the fire pot, where they ignite to produce heat and smoke. The cooking chamber is where the magic happens, and understanding how these parts work together will enhance your overall cooking proficiency.

Choosing the Right Pellets

The type of wood pellets you use significantly influences the flavor of your food. Different woods impart distinct flavors, ranging from mild to robust. For a mild, versatile flavor, consider using fruitwood pellets like apple or cherry. If you prefer a stronger, smokier taste, opt for hickory or mesquite pellets. Experiment with different wood blends to discover your preferred flavor profile.

Maintaining Consistent Temperatures

Pellet grills are renowned for their ability to maintain consistent temperatures, but achieving this requires proper operation. Start by preheating your grill to the

desired temperature before placing the food on the grates. Avoid frequently opening the lid, as this can cause temperature fluctuations. Additionally, keep the lid closed as much as possible during the cooking process to retain heat and smoke.

Understanding Direct and Indirect Heat

Pellet grills offer both direct and indirect cooking options. Direct heat is suitable for quick-cooking items like burgers and steaks, while indirect heat is ideal for slow-cooking larger cuts of meat. Familiarize yourself with the different zones on your grill, allowing you to utilize direct or indirect heat as needed for various recipes.

Using a Meat Probe

Investing in a quality meat probe is a game-changer for pellet grill enthusiasts. This tool helps you monitor the internal temperature of your food, ensuring it reaches the desired level of doneness. Insert the probe into the thickest part of the meat, away from bones, to get an accurate reading. This prevents overcooking or undercooking and guarantees a perfectly cooked meal every time.

Maintaining and Cleaning Your Pellet Grill

Proper maintenance is crucial for the longevity and efficiency of your Pit

Boss pellet grill. Regularly clean the grates and grease tray to prevent flare-ups and maintain optimal performance. Empty the ash pot after each use to ensure proper airflow. Additionally, follow the manufacturer's guidelines for more in-depth cleaning and maintenance tasks.

Experimenting with Recipes

Once you've mastered the basics, don't be afraid to experiment with different recipes and cooking techniques. Pellet grills are incredibly versatile, allowing you to smoke, grill, roast, and even bake. Whether you're smoking a brisket, grilling vegetables, or baking a pizza, the possibilities are endless. Start with simple recipes and gradually challenge yourself to try more complex dishes.

Joining the Pellet Grilling Community

Pellet grilling has a vibrant and supportive community of enthusiasts sharing tips, recipes, and experiences. Join online forums, social media groups, or local barbecue clubs to connect with fellow pellet grill aficionados. This community can provide valuable insights, troubleshooting tips, and inspiration for your culinary adventures.

In conclusion, mastering pellet grilling with a Pit Boss grill involves understanding the equipment, choosing the right pellets, maintaining consistent temperatures, utilizing direct and indirect heat, using a meat probe, cleaning and maintaining the grill, experimenting with recipes, and joining the vibrant community of pellet grilling enthusiasts. With these tips, you'll be well on your way to becoming a confident and skilled pellet grill chef, ready to impress friends and family with delicious and perfectly cooked dishes.

Set the Right Temperature of Cooking and Smoking

Setting the right temperature when cooking or smoking with a Pit Boss Grill is crucial for achieving the desired results. Whether you're grilling a steak, smoking brisket, or slow-cooking ribs, the temperature control plays a significant role in the final flavor and texture of your dish.

Pit Boss Grills typically come with a temperature control system that allows you to adjust the heat easily. The optimal temperature varies depending on the type of meat and the cooking method. Let's delve into the specifics of setting the right temperature for various cooking scenarios:

- Grilling Steaks:

When grilling steaks on a Pit Boss Grill, you'll want to achieve a high temperature to sear the outside while keeping the inside juicy. Preheat your grill to a temperature between 400°F and 450°F for the perfect sear. Searing locks in the juices and creates a flavorful crust on the steak. After searing, reduce the temperature to around 350°F to finish cooking the steak to your desired doneness.

- Smoking Brisket:

Smoking brisket is a slow and low process that imparts a rich, smoky flavor. Set your Pit Boss Grill to a low temperature between 225°F and 250°F for smoking. This low and slow method allows the collagen in the brisket to break down, resulting in a tender and flavorful end product. Maintain a consistent temperature throughout the smoking process to ensure even cooking and a succulent final result.

- Slow-Cooking Ribs:

For slow-cooking ribs on a Pit Boss Grill, aim for a temperature range of 225°F to 250°F. This low temperature allows the ribs to cook slowly,

becoming tender and developing a smoky flavor. You can use the 3-2-1 method for baby back ribs, where you smoke them for 3 hours, wrap in foil and cook for 2 more hours, then unwrap and cook for a final hour. Adjust the temperature as needed to achieve the desired tenderness and flavor.

- Poultry:

  Poultry, such as chicken or turkey, benefits from a higher initial temperature for a crispy skin. Preheat your Pit Boss Grill to around 375°F to 400°F when cooking poultry. Once you achieve a golden-brown skin, reduce the temperature to 325°F for the remainder of the cooking time. This method ensures that the poultry is thoroughly cooked while maintaining a crispy exterior.

- Pizza:

  Pit Boss Grills are versatile and can be used for cooking more than just traditional barbecue fare. When making pizza, preheat the grill to a high temperature of around 500°F to 550°F. This high heat helps create a crispy crust and perfectly melted toppings. Keep a close eye on the pizza to prevent burning, as the cooking time is relatively short at such high temperatures.

In conclusion, setting the right temperature for your Pit Boss Grill is essential for achieving the best results in your cooking endeavors. Whether you're grilling, smoking, slow-cooking, or making pizza, understanding the optimal temperature ranges for each type of dish will elevate your culinary creations and make you a master of your Pit Boss Grill. Adjusting the temperature according to the specific requirements of each recipe will ensure that you consistently produce delicious and perfectly cooked meals for your family and friends.

Best Tools And Supplies To Improve Your Smoking And Grilling

Mastering the art of smoking and grilling requires not only skill but also the right tools and supplies. Pit Boss Grills, known for their versatility and performance, can be enhanced further with the following essential tools and supplies to elevate your outdoor cooking experience.

Quality Meat Thermometer

One of the keys to successful smoking and grilling is precision, especially when it comes to cooking meat. A high-quality meat thermometer is a must-have tool to ensure your food is cooked to perfection. Look for a digital thermometer with a probe to accurately monitor the internal temperature of your meat. This prevents overcooking or undercooking and guarantees a juicy and flavorful result every time.

Cast Iron Grates and Skillets

Upgrade your Pit Boss Grill by investing in cast iron grates and skillets. These add versatility to your cooking by providing excellent heat retention and distribution. Cast iron grates are perfect for achieving those beautiful grill marks on steaks and burgers, while cast iron skillets are ideal for searing and sautéing. Seasoning them properly also adds a unique flavor to your dishes.

Smoking Wood Chips and Pellets

The heart of smoking is the flavor infusion from wood chips or pellets. Experiment with different types of wood, such as hickory, mesquite, apple, or cherry, to discover the perfect complement to your meats. Pit Boss Grills are designed to work with various wood flavors, allowing you to achieve a distinctive smoky taste that enhances the overall dining experience.

Heat-Resistant Gloves

Handling hot grates, adjusting vents, or placing wood chips into the firebox can be challenging without the right protection. Heat-resistant gloves are indispensable for the serious griller. Look for gloves that are not only heat-resistant but also provide dexterity to handle tasks with precision. This ensures safety while allowing you to maintain control over the grilling process.

Grill Brush and Scraper

Keeping your Pit Boss Grill clean is essential for maintaining optimal performance and preventing flare-ups. Invest in a high-quality grill brush with a scraper to remove residue and grease from the grates. Regular cleaning not only extends the life of your grill but also ensures that each meal is cooked on a clean surface, free from unwanted flavors or contaminants.

Drip Pan Liners

Simplify cleanup after a grilling session by using drip pan liners. These disposable liners fit seamlessly into the drip pan of your Pit Boss Grill, collecting grease and drippings. Not only do they make cleaning more convenient, but they also help prevent flare-ups and reduce the risk of grease fires. Ensure you choose liners that are compatible with your specific Pit Boss model.

Wireless Meat Probe Thermometer

For added convenience, consider a wireless meat probe thermometer. This tool allows you to monitor the temperature of your meat remotely, providing the flexibility to socialize with guests or attend to other tasks while ensuring your food is cooking as intended. Some models even connect to mobile apps, allowing you to receive temperature alerts and track the progress of your cook from your smartphone.

Conclusion

Elevating your smoking and grilling game on Pit Boss Grills involves more than just culinary skill—it requires the right tools and supplies. From precision temperature control to flavor-enhancing wood chips, investing in quality accessories ensures a seamless and enjoyable outdoor cooking experience. Equip yourself with these essentials, and watch as your Pit Boss Grill becomes the centerpiece of unforgettable meals and gatherings.

Chapter 1: Rub and Sauces

Southwestern Style Smoked Red Chili Hot Sauce

Prep Time: 20 Minutes   Cook Time: 1 Hour 30 Minutes   Serves: 3

Ingredients:

- 15 red jalapeno peppers, seeds removed
- 1 cup yellow onion diced
- 2 tablespoons fresh garlic, chopped
- 2 tablespoons ground cumin
- 2 tablespoons dry oregano
- 2 teaspoons kosher salt
- 2 tablespoons tomato paste
- 2 tablespoons molasses
- 2 tablespoons cider vinegar

Directions:

1. Preheat your Pit Boss Pellet Grill to 225°F, let it heat for 5 to 10 minutes while prepping your chilis.
2. On a cutting board, remove the tops and slice the chilis in half while wearing gloves. Remove the seeds from the chilis.
3. Place the peppers on the grill with the sliced side faced down towards the heat source. Smoke at 225°F for 45 minutes to 1 hour.
4. Remove the peppers from the grill. Place the peppers and the remaining ingredients along with 2.5 cups of water in a large pot and cover.
5. Place the pot on a stove and bring to a boil. Once it reaches a boil, turn down and let it simmer for 15 to 25 minutes. The peppers should be nice and soft and over half of the water should have evaporated.
6. Remove from heat and allow it to cool before pouring the mixture into a food processor.
7. Process until the mixture is nice and smooth.
8. Add molasses and vinegar and mix.
9. Place a strainer on top of a bucket or pot and pour the contents in the food processor over the strainer to remove any remaining solids.
10. Pour the hot sauce into a bottle or jar and enjoy. It should keep in your refrigerator for at least a few months!

Nutritional Value (Amount per Serving):

Calories: 191; Fat: 4.53; Carb: 37.44; Protein: 5.2

Louisiana Style Smoked Hot Sauce

Prep Time: 15 Minutes   Cook Time: 1 Hour 15 Minutes   Serves: 4-5

Ingredients:

- 1 pound Serrano peppers, seeds removed
- 1 quart water
- 1 teaspoon salt

- ½ cup red vinegar

Directions:

1. Preheat your Pit Boss Pellet Grill to 225°F, let it heat for 5 to 10 minutes while prepping your chilis
2. On a cutting board, remove the tops and slice the chilis in half while wearing gloves. Remove the seeds from the chilis.
3. Place the peppers on the grill with the sliced side faced down towards the heat source. Smoke at 225°F for 45 minutes to 1 hour.
4. Remove the peppers from the grill. Place the peppers and the remaining ingredients in a large pot and cover.
5. Place the pot on a stove and bring to a boil. Once it reaches a boil, turn down and let it simmer for 10 to 15 minutes. The peppers should be nice and soft.
6. Remove from heat and allow it to cool before pouring the mixture into a food processor.
7. Process until the mixture is nice and smooth. You may have to do multiple batches depending on how large your food processor is.
8. Place a strainer on top of a bucket or pot and pour the contents of the food processor over the strainer to remove any remaining solids.
9. Pour the hot sauce into a bottle or jar and enjoy. It should keep in your refrigerator for at least a few months.

Nutritional Value (Amount per Serving):

Calories: 34; Fat: 0.4; Carb: 6.14; Protein: 1.59

Sweet BBQ Sauce

Prep Time: 5 Minutes   Cook Time: 30 Minutes   Serves: 4

Ingredients:

- 1 ½ cups ketchup
- 1 ½ cups brown sugar
- 1/2 cup apple cider vinegar
- 1/2 cup water
- 1 tbsp Worcestershire sauce
- 1 tbsp molasses
- 1 ½ tbsp dry mustard
- 1 tbsp paprika
- 1/2 tbsp salt
- 1/2 tsp onion powder
- ½ tbsp black pepper
- 2 dashes hot sauce

Directions:

1. In a sauce pan combine all of the ingredients until well blended.
2. Preheat you Pit Boss Grill to 225°F.
3. Cook over low heat to marry all of the flavors together. About 20 -30 minutes. This step can be optional, but it does help to develop the sauce.
4. Give your sauce a taste. You may choose to add a little more vinegar or

seasonings depending on your personal taste.

Nutritional Value (Amount per Serving):

Calories: 452; Fat: 0.6; Carb: 116.66; Protein: 1.86

Honey BBQ Sauce

Prep Time: 5 Minutes   Cook Time: 1 Hour   Serves: 12

Ingredients:

- 1 cup ketchup
- ½ cup honey
- ⅓ cup brown sugar
- ¼ cup white wine vinegar
- 1 teaspoon salt
- 1 teaspoon smoked paprika
- 1 teaspoon onion powder
- 1 teaspoon garlic powder
- ½ teaspoon pepper

Directions:

1. Combine the ingredients in a pan, and stir to combine.
2. Preheat your Pit Boss Grill to 225°F.
3. Cook the sauce about 40-60 minutes, or until it has thickened to your liking.
4. Stir occasionally while the sauce is cooking to prevent it from burning.
5. Allow the sauce to cool down before transferring it to a container for storage.

Nutritional Value (Amount per Serving):

Calories: 90; Fat: 0.05; Carb: 23.73; Protein: 0.39

Spicy BBQ Sauce

Prep Time: 10 Minutes   Cook Time: 8 Minutes   Serves: 8

Ingredients:

- 1 cup ketchup
- 1 cup dark brown sugar
- ¼ cup molasses
- ¼ cup pineapple juice
- ¼ cup water
- 1 tablespoon tomato paste
- 1 tablespoon worcestershire sauce
- 1 tablespoon Creole seasoning
- 1 tablespoon Cajun seasoning
- 2 ½ teaspoons ground mustard

- 2 teaspoons smoked paprika
- 1 ½ teaspoons coarse kosher salt
- 1 teaspoon freshly ground black pepper
- ½ teaspoon garlic powder
- ¼ teaspoon cayenne pepper
- ⅛ cup cold water mixed with 1 tablespoon cornstarch

Directions:

1. Combine all ingredients except the cornstarch mixture in a medium sized sauce pan.
2. Preheat your Pit Boss Grill to 220°F.
3. Simmer for five minutes or until the sugar has dissolved.
4. Add the cornstarch mixture and simmer until desired thickness is reached, a few more minutes.
5. Serve immediately or transfer to a covered container and store in the fridge.

Nutritional Value (Amount per Serving):

Calories: 131; Fat: 0.38; Carb: 32.8; Protein: 0.85

Texas Style BBQ Sauce

Prep Time: 10 Minutes   Cook Time: 20 Minutes   Serves: 4

Ingredients:

- 15 ounces tomato sauce canned
- ½ cup apple juice
- ¼ cup apple cider vinegar
- ¼ cup packed dark brown sugar
- 2 tablespoons molasses
- 1 tablespoon worcestershire sauce
- 1 tablespoon onion powder
- 2 teaspoons garlic powder
- 1 teaspoon prepared mustard
- ¼-½ teaspoon cayenne pepper

Directions:

1. In a medium sauce pan, combine all the ingredients.
2. Preheat your Pit Boss grill to 225°F.
3. Simmer over low heat for 20 minutes.
4. Stir the ingredients often while cooking.
5. Once the sauce has finished cooking, then remove it from the heat.
6. Allow it to cool.

Nutritional Value (Amount per Serving):

Calories: 201; Fat: 0.49; Carb: 43.5; Protein: 3.21

Kentucky Kandy BBQ Sauce

Prep Time: 10 Minutes   Cook Time: 20 Minutes   Serves: 4-5

Ingredients:

- 1 tbsp olive oil (extra virgin)
- 2 cloves garlic (minced)
- 2 tsp chili power
- ½ tsp ground cumin
- ½ tsp black pepper
- ¾ cup ketchup
- ½ cup coke
- ⅔ cup dark brown sugar
- 2 tbsp soy sauce
- 2 tbsp apple cider vinegar
- 2 tbsp bourbon
- 1 tsp liquid smoke

Directions:

1. Preheat your Pit Boss grill to 225°F.
2. Add the garlic, chili powder, cumin, and black pepper.
3. Cook for about 30 seconds, stirring constantly and remove from heat.
4. Whisk in the remaining ingredients, return to heat, and simmer for about 15-20 min, stirring occasionally.
5. For a smooth sauce, you can either blend it or pour through a strainer while still warm.
6. Let cool and refrigerate.

Nutritional Value (Amount per Serving):

Calories: 164; Fat: 4.69; Carb: 30.08; Protein: 1.39

KFC Honey BBQ Sauce

Prep Time: 5 Minutes   Cook Time: 20 Minutes   Serves: 2

Ingredients:

- 6 ounces tomato paste
- ½ cup water + 1-2 more Tablespoons (optional)
- 2 tablespoons apple cider vinegar or white vinegar
- ¼ cup dark brown sugar
- ¼ cup honey
- 1 teaspoon hickory flavored liquid smoke
- 1 teaspoon
- ½ teaspoon onion powder
- ½ teaspoon garlic powder
- ¼ teaspoon ground celery
- ¼ teaspoon paprika
- 1 pinch cayenne pepper optional

Directions:

1. Preheat your Pit Boss grill to 225°F.
2. Combine all the ingredients in a saucepan. If too thick for your liking, add the additional 1-2 tablespoons of water.

3. Stir until ingredients are well combined and bring to a boil.
4. Once boiling, reduce heat and simmer uncovered for 15-20 minutes.
5. Serve and enjoy!

Nutritional Value (Amount per Serving):

Calories: 275; Fat: 0.85; Carb: 69.48; Protein: 4.52

Sweet Baby Ray's BBQ Sauce

Prep Time: 5 Minutes   Cook Time: 10 Minutes   Serves: 4

Ingredients:

- 1 ⅓ cup ketchup
- ¾ cup brown sugar
- ¼ cup molasses
- 1 (6-ounce) can pineapple juice (preferably no sugar added)
- 2 tablespoons each: Worcestershire sauce and apple cider vinegar
- 1 tablespoon each: dry mustard powder and smoked paprika
- 2 teaspoons cornstarch
- 1 teaspoon each: garlic powder, salt and hot sauce (any kind you like)
- ½ teaspoon each: black pepper and onion powder
- ¼ teaspoon cayenne pepper, optional

Directions:

1. Add ⅓ cup water along with all the ingredients listed to a saucepan and whisk until smooth.
2. When all the lumps have been worked out, preheat your Pit Boss grill to 230°F.
3. When it starts bubbling, lower the heat so it just simmers and allow it to cook for 5-7 minutes until it thickens.
4. Brush on meats or poultry when grilling, as a sauce for pizza, or as a base for dips and dressings.

Nutritional Value (Amount per Serving):

Calories: 474; Fat: 1.55; Carb: 111.85; Protein: 7.8

Root Beer BBQ Sauce

Prep Time: 10 Minutes   Cook Time: 20 Minutes   Serves: 5

Ingredients:

- 1 cup root beer
- 1 cup ketchup
- 1/4 c lemon juice
- 1/4 c orange juice

- 3 T worcestershire
- 1 1/2 T dark brown sugar
- 1 T light molasses
- 1 tsp liquid smoke
- 1/2 tsp lemon zest
- 1/2 tsp ground ginger
- 1/2 tsp garlic powder
- 1/2 tsp onion powder

Directions:

1. Preheat your Pit Boss grill to 230°F.
2. Place all ingredients in a small saucepan.
3. Whisk together, then simmer on medium-low until the mixture has reduced to approximately 1 1/2 cups, about 20 min.
4. Stir frequently to keep from burning.

Nutritional Value (Amount per Serving):

Calories: 115; Fat: 0.67; Carb: 28.63; Protein: 0.96

Carolina Barbecue Sauce

Prep Time: 5 Minutes   Cook Time: 10 Minutes   Serves: 4

Ingredients:

- 1 cup ketchup
- 1/2 cup yellow mustard
- 1/2 cup brown sugar
- 1 cup apple cider vinegar
- 1 tbsp. olive oil
- 2 tsp. Worcestershire sauce
- 1 tsp. paprika
- 1/4 tsp. Cayenne pepper
- 2 tsp. ground mustard
- 1 tsp. garlic powder

Directions:

1. Preheat your Pit Boss grill to 350°F.
2. Combine everything in a large saucepan.
3. Reduce heat to medium low and stir frequently for 5 minutes, sauce will reduce by a third.
4. Allow to cool slightly and store in an airtight container for up to 3 weeks.

Nutritional Value (Amount per Serving):

Calories: 254; Fat: 5.02; Carb: 54.02; Protein: 2.37

Smoky Maple BBQ Sauce

Prep Time: 15 Minutes   Cook Time: 30 Minutes   Serves: 8

Ingredients:

- 1 cup ketchup
- 1/2 cup apple cider vinegar
- 1/4 cup maple syrup
- 2 tablespoons Worcestershire sauce
- 1 tablespoon Dijon mustard
- 1 teaspoon smoked paprika

- 1 teaspoon garlic powder
- Salt and black pepper to taste

Directions:

1. In a medium saucepan, combine ketchup, apple cider vinegar, maple syrup, Worcestershire sauce, Dijon mustard, smoked paprika, and garlic powder.
2. Preheat your Pit Boss grill to 300°F.
3. Stir well to combine all the ingredients.
4. Reduce the heat to low and let the sauce simmer for about 20-25 minutes, stirring occasionally. Allow the flavors to meld, and the sauce to thicken to your desired consistency. Season with salt and black pepper to taste.
5. Remove the saucepan from heat and let the BBQ sauce cool to room temperature. Transfer it to a clean, airtight container for storage.

Note: During the last 10 minutes of grilling your meat, generously brush the smoky maple BBQ sauce onto the surface, allowing it to caramelize and create a flavorful glaze.

Note: Serve your grilled meat with an extra side of smoky maple BBQ sauce for dipping. The sweet and savory flavors will enhance the smokiness from the grill.

Nutritional Value (Amount per Serving):

Calories: 72; Fat: 0.17; Carb: 18.48; Protein: 0.62

Tangy Mustard BBQ Sauce

Prep Time: 10 Minutes   Cook Time: 15 Minutes   Serves: 8

Ingredients:

- 1 cup yellow mustard
- 1/2 cup apple cider vinegar
- 1/4 cup honey
- 2 tablespoons brown sugar
- 1 tablespoon hot sauce
- 1 teaspoon onion powder
- 1 teaspoon garlic powder
- Salt and black pepper to taste

Directions:

1. In a saucepan, whisk together yellow mustard, apple cider vinegar, honey, brown sugar, hot sauce, onion powder, and garlic powder.
2. Preheat the grill to 300°F.
3. Cook the mixture over medium heat, stirring frequently.
4. Simmer for about 10 minutes until the sauce thickens slightly.
5. Season with salt and black pepper to taste.
6. Let it cool before transferring to a jar. Use as a dipping sauce or glaze for grilled meats.

Nutritional Value (Amount per Serving):

Calories: 66; Fat: 1.08; Carb: 14.17; Protein: 1.43

Honey Chipotle BBQ Sauce

Prep Time: 15 Minutes   Cook Time: 20 Minutes   Serves: 8

Ingredients:

- 1 cup ketchup
- 1/2 cup honey
- 2 chipotle peppers in adobo sauce, minced
- 2 tablespoons apple cider vinegar
- 1 tablespoon Dijon mustard
- 1 teaspoon onion powder
- 1 teaspoon garlic powder
- Salt to taste

Directions:

1. In a saucepan, combine ketchup, honey, minced chipotle peppers, apple cider vinegar, Dijon mustard, onion powder, and garlic powder.
2. Preheat the Pit Boss grill to 320°F.
3. Simmer for about 15 minutes until the sauce thickens, stirring continuously.
4. Season with salt to taste and let it cool before using.

Nutritional Value (Amount per Serving):

Calories: 104; Fat: 0.13; Carb: 27.81; Protein: 0.77

Pineapple Teriyaki Glaze

Prep Time: 10 Minutes   Cook Time: 15 Minutes   Serves: 8

Ingredients:

- 1 cup pineapple juice
- 1/4 cup soy sauce
- 2 tablespoons brown sugar
- 1 tablespoon rice vinegar
- 1 teaspoon garlic powder
- 1 teaspoon ginger, grated
- 1 tablespoon cornstarch (optional, for thickening)

Directions:

1. In a saucepan, combine pineapple juice, soy sauce, brown sugar, rice vinegar, garlic powder, and grated ginger.
2. Preheat the Pit Boss grill to 320°F.
3. Optional: If you prefer a thicker glaze, mix cornstarch with a little water to make a slurry and stir it into the sauce.

4. Simmer for about 10 minutes until the sauce thickens.

5. Let it cool before using as a glaze for grilled meats.

Nutritional Value (Amount per Serving):

Calories: 51; Fat: 1.47; Carb: 8.91; Protein: 0.77

Roasted Red Pepper Sauce

Prep Time: 15 Minutes   Cook Time: 25 Minutes   Serves: 6

Ingredients:

- 2 large red bell peppers, roasted and peeled
- 1/2 cup tomato sauce
- 2 cloves garlic, minced
- 1 tablespoon olive oil
- 1 teaspoon dried basil
- Salt and black pepper to taste

Directions:

1. Roast red bell peppers until the skin is charred. Peel and remove seeds.
2. In a blender, combine roasted red peppers, tomato sauce, minced garlic, olive oil, dried basil, salt, and black pepper.
3. Blend until smooth.
4. Preheat the grill to 300°F.
5. Transfer the mixture to a saucepan and simmer for about 10 minutes.
6. Cool before serving as a dipping sauce or glaze.

Nutritional Value (Amount per Serving):

Calories: 54; Fat: 2.37; Carb: 7.02; Protein: 1.11

Mango Habanero BBQ Sauce

Prep Time: 15 Minutes   Cook Time: 20 Minutes   Serves: 8-10

Ingredients:

- 1 cup mango, diced
- 1/2 cup ketchup
- 1/4 cup apple cider vinegar
- 2 tablespoons honey
- 1 habanero pepper, seeded and minced
- 1 tablespoon soy sauce
- 1 teaspoon ginger, grated
- Salt to taste

Directions:

1. In a blender, combine diced mango, ketchup, apple cider vinegar, honey,

habanero pepper, soy sauce, and grated ginger.
2. Blend until smooth.
3. Preheat the Pit Boss grill to 300°F.
4. Pour the mixture into a saucepan and simmer for about 15 minutes until the sauce thickens.
5. Season with salt to taste.
6. Allow the sauce to cool before using as a glaze for grilled meats.

Nutritional Value (Amount per Serving):

Calories: 49; Fat: 0.42; Carb: 11.98; Protein: 0.54

Cherry Balsamic Glaze

Prep Time: 10 Minutes   Cook Time: 20 Minutes   Serves: 8-10

Ingredients:

- 1 cup fresh or frozen cherries, pitted
- 1/2 cup balsamic vinegar
- 1/4 cup brown sugar
- 1 tablespoon soy sauce
- 1 teaspoon rosemary, chopped
- 1 teaspoon cornstarch (optional, for thickening)
- Salt to taste

Directions:

1. In a blender, combine pitted cherries, balsamic vinegar, brown sugar, soy sauce, and chopped rosemary.
2. Blend until smooth.
3. Preheat the grill to 300°F.
4. Pour the mixture into a saucepan and simmer for about 15 minutes until the cherries break down and the sauce thickens.
5. Optional: If you prefer a thicker glaze, mix cornstarch with a little water to make a slurry and stir it into the sauce.
6. Season with salt to taste.
7. Allow the glaze to cool before using it to enhance the flavor of grilled meats.

Nutritional Value (Amount per Serving):

Calories: 68; Fat: 0.36; Carb: 15.57; Protein: 0.54

Chapter 2: Beef and Lamb

Chipotle Lamb

Prep Time: 30 Minutes   Cook Time: 30 Minutes   Serves: 6

Ingredients:

- Black pepper
- 3/4 cup Extra-Virgin olive oil
- 2 tbsp Italian Parsley
- 1/4 cup Pit Boss Rub
- 2 tbsp sage, fresh
- 1 tbsp Chipotle peppers, crushed
- 3 garlic, cloves
- 1 rack lamb ribs
- 2 tbsp rosemary, fresh
- 2 tbsp thyme, fresh sprigs

Directions:

1. For the dry rub baste the lamb ribs with olive oil and season with the chipotle powder and black pepper. Let the lamb ribs rest for at least 15 minutes in the refrigerator.
2. Preheat your Pit Boss Grill to 275°F.
3. For the wet rub Blend rosemary, cilantro, Italian parsley, sage, thyme, and oregano with ¼ cup Extra Virgin Olive Oil, ¼ cup of Pit Boss Rub and 2-3 garlic cloves.
4. Apply the wet rub all over the lamb ribs.
5. Lay your lamb ribs bone side down on the grill and smoke until they reach an internal temp of 120°F to 125°F.
6. Turn your grill temp up to 425°F and sear until internal temp of 135°F to 145°F.
7. Rest 10-15 minutes. Carve and enjoy!

Nutritional Value (Amount per Serving):

Calories: 151; Fat: 14.07; Carb: 4.31; Protein: 2.38

Grilled Rack of Lamb

Prep Time: 25 Minutes   Cook Time: 30 Minutes   Serves: 8

Ingredients:

- 2 tbsp Dijon mustard
- Pit Boss Chop House Steak Rub
- 1 tsp rosemary, finely chopped
- 1 tbsp fresh parsley, chopped
- 2 chine bones removed, and excess fat trimmed racks of lamb

Directions:

1. Place the racks of lamb on a flat work surface, then generously brush the lamb all over with Dijon mustard.
2. Season the meat on all sides with Pit Boss Chophouse Steak Rub and sprinkle with parsley and rosemary.
3. Preheat your Pit Boss Grill to 400°F.

4. Insert a temperature probe into the thickest part of the rack of lamb and sear the rack, meaty side down for about 6 minutes.
5. Remove the lamb from the grill and turn the temperature down to 300°F.
6. Return the lamb to the grill and lean the two racks against each other so that they stand up, and grill for another 20 minutes, or until the internal temperature reaches 130°F.
7. Remove the racks from the grill and allow to rest for 10 minutes before carving and serving.

Nutritional Value (Amount per Serving):

Calories: 236; Fat: 14.98; Carb: 0.55; Protein: 23.32

Lamb Rack with Rosemary Mint Compound Butter

Prep Time: 15 Minutes   Cook Time: 25 Minutes   Serves: 2

Ingredients:

- 1/2 lb. softened butter
- 1 oz fresh mint
- 1 1/2 tsp fresh rosemary, chopped
- 1 tsp salt
- 1/2 tsp onion powder
- 1/2 tsp garlic powder
- 1 tsp Dijon mustard
- 14-16 oz rack of lamb
- Pit Boss smoked salt & pepper rub

Directions:

1. Preheat your Pit Boss Grill to 300°F.
2. Meanwhile, combine softened butter, rosemary, mint, salt, onion powder, garlic powder, and mustard in a bowl, and set aside.
3. Next, apply the binder of your choice to the lamb, and season it with the Pit Boss Smokey Salt and Cracked Pepper Rub.
4. Then, open the flame broiler, place the Lamb directly on the grates, and direct-sear over an open flame for about 2-3 mins on each side.
5. Once your lamb has been seared, close the flame broiler, and cook for about 20-25 mins, or until you reach an internal temperature of 135-137°F.
6. Remove from the grill, let rest, and slice.
7. Finally, top with fresh rosemary mint compound butter and enjoy.

Nutritional Value (Amount per Serving):

Calories: 1235; Fat: 112.2; Carb: 12.86; Protein: 48.39

Beef Rack Ribs

Prep Time: 20 Minutes   Cook Time: 4 Hours 30 Minutes   Serves: 4

Ingredients:

- 2 sides beef back ribs
- Pit Boss GSP Rub
- 1 cup "Spritz": 2 parts Worcestershire, 1 part lime juice

Directions:

1. Preheat your Pit Boss Grill to 225°F
2. While your grill is heating up, peel the membrane off the beef back ribs, and season the ribs with Pit Boss GSP on all sides.
3. Next, place your beef back ribs directly on the grates of the smoker, and smoke for 2.5 hours. Be sure to spritz every half hour for best results.
4. After 2 1/2 hours of smoking at 225°F, pull the ribs off the smoker, and coat them with soft butter. Once coated, wrap the ribs with butcher paper.
5. Then, place the ribs back on the smoker at 275°F for another 11/2 to 2 hours.
6. Remove the ribs from the smoker, and allow to rest for at least 10 minutes.
7. If desired, glaze with BBQ sauce and place back on the smoker for 20 minutes.
8. Remove from the smoker, slice, and enjoy!

Nutritional Value (Amount per Serving):

Calories: 1747; Fat: 122.91; Carb: 8.15; Protein: 154.24

Baebecue Stuffed Beef Can Burgers

Prep Time: 10 Minutes   Cook Time: 1 Hour   Serves: 4

Ingredients:

- 8 bacon slices
- 1/2 lb Cheddar jack, cubed
- 1 Jalapeno pepper, minced
- 1 white onion, caramelized
- 1 beer, Can
- 2 1/2 lbs ground beef
- Pit Boss sweet rib rub

Directions:

1. Preheat your Pit Boss Grill to 300°F.
2. Place ground beef in a mixing bowl, season with Pit Boss Sweet Rib Rub, then mix by hand.
3. Form 4, 10 ounces balls, then use a can (any 12 ounces aluminum can will work), and press the can down the center of each ball, creating a small beef bowl.
4. Press along the sides and roll to create a beef bowl, approximately 3 ½ inches tall.
5. Wrap beef with 2 pieces of bacon, then fill with cheese, caramelized onion,

and minced jalapeño.

6. Set filled burgers in a large cast iron skillet, then transfer to the grill.
7. Cook for 25 minutes in the skillet, then transfer burgers to the top rack.
8. Increase the temperature to 325°F, and cook an additional 25 to 30 minutes, rotating halfway.
9. Remove from the grill, top with extra jalapeño, rest for 5 minutes, then serve warm.

Nutritional Value (Amount per Serving):

Calories: 1441; Fat: 96.3; Carb: 47.29; Protein: 91.66

Bacon Wrapped Steaks

Prep Time: 10 Minutes   Cook Time: 15 Minutes   Serves: 4

Ingredients:

- 2 tbsp Pit Boss All Purpose GSP Rub
- 3 1/2 tsp chives, chopped
- 1/4 cup olive oil
- 4, (6-7 oz) 1 inch thick steaks
- 3 tbsp unsalted butter, melted
- 1/2 tsp dried thyme, fresh sprigs

Directions:

1. Preheat your Pit Boss Grill to 425°F. While your grill is heating up, mix the melted butter, olive oil, Pit Boss All Purpose GSP Rub, chives, and thyme into a bowl.
2. Wrap the bacon around the sides of the steaks and hold in place with a toothpick.
3. Baste the top and bottom of the steaks with the mix using a basting brush.
4. Place the steaks on the grill and brown for 5 minutes on each side.
5. Remove steaks once internal temperature has reached the level of desired doneness: Rare (120°F), Medium Rare (130°F), Medium (140°F), Well Done (160°F).
6. After removing the steaks, let them rest for at least 5 minutes.

Nutritional Value (Amount per Serving):

Calories: 680; Fat: 52.06; Carb: 3.04; Protein: 47.16

Cheesy Stuffed Steak Rolls

Prep Time: 20 Minutes   Cook Time: 10 Minutes   Serves: 4

Ingredients:

- 4 oz cream cheese, softened
- 1 1/4 lbs flank steak

- Pit Boss Chop House Steak Rub
- 1/4 cup sour cream
- 1 tbsp sun dried tomatoes, minced
- 1/4 tsp fennel, ground
- 2 tbsp olive oil
- 6 slices Provolone cheese, sliced
- 1 cup spinach, chopped

Directions:

1. Preheat your Pit Boss Grill to 425°F.
2. Place flank steak on a cutting board and slice horizontally across, to open, without completely cutting through. Use a meat mallet to pound to even thickness, if needed.
3. Season the steak on both sides evenly with Pit Boss Chophouse Steak Rub. Set aside.
4. In a mixing bowl, use a hand mixer to combine cream cheese, sour cream, sun dried tomatoes, and fennel.
5. Spread cream cheese mixture on steak, then layer spinach and provolone. Roll steak, then tie with kitchen twine every 2 inches. Slice steak in between ties to cut into individual portions.
6. On the griddle top, carefully add oil and heat.
7. Add steak rolls and sear 5 minutes per side.
8. Remove steaks from the grill and allow to rest for 5 minutes. Serve warm.

Nutritional Value (Amount per Serving):

Calories: 527; Fat: 35.26; Carb: 7.68; Protein: 43.74

Corned Beef & Cabbage

Prep Time: 10 Minutes   Cook Time: 5 Hours   Serves: 4

Ingredients:

- 3 lbs flat cut corned beef brisket
- 1 green cabbage
- 1 red cabbage
- 5 red potatoes
- 48 oz. beef broth
- Pit Boss Alberta Black Gold Rub

Directions:

1. Preheat your Pit Boss Grill or Smoker to 200°F.
2. Season corn beef with Pit Boss Alberta Black Gold Rub.
3. Place corn beef in cast iron skillet then pour beef broth to submerge meat. Place in the smoker over the heat source with grates open. Let cook for 3 hours.
4. While the corned beef cooks, prep the vegetables. Cut the cabbage into quarters with the core cut out, then clean potatoes.
5. After the third hour passes, open the lid, and place all the vegetables into the skillet and cook for another 2 hours.
6. Finally, the time has come. Remove cast iron from smoker and take corn

beef out to rest. Cut yourself a piece and dig in!

Nutritional Value (Amount per Serving):

Calories: 948; Fat: 18.78; Carb: 113.93; Protein: 85.75

Cowboy Nachos

Prep Time: 20 Minutes   Cook Time: 20 Minutes   Serves: 8

Ingredients:

- Cilantro
- Olive oil
- 1 red bell peppers, sliced
- 2 rib-eye steaks
- Salsa
- 1 tbsp Pit Boss All Purpose GSP
- 1 cup Shredded Cheddar Cheese
- Sour cream
- 1 yellow bell pepper, sliced
- 1 zucchini, sliced

Directions:

1. Preheat your Pit Boss grill to 400°F.
2. Coat both sides of the steak with olive oil and season with Pit Boss All Purpose GSP. Place the steak on the grates and grill for about 4 to 5 minutes per side.
3. Remove the steak off the grill and let rest for about 10 minutes before cutting into bite-sized strips.
4. Brush with barbecue sauce if desired.
5. Empty a large bag of nacho chips evenly into a cast iron pan. Start loading up with toppings - steak, cheddar cheese, sautéed vegetables.
6. These are just suggested toppings, so feel free to add anything you like!
7. Place your loaded nachos on the grill and let the hot smoke melt your toppings into one hearty creation.
8. Cook for about 10 minutes, or until the cheese has fully melted.
9. Remove and serve with sour cream and salsa.

Nutritional Value (Amount per Serving):

Calories: 380; Fat: 29.9; Carb: 4.6; Protein: 23.61

Cowboy Ribeye Steak

Prep Time: 5 Minutes   Cook Time: 1 Hour   Serves: 2

Ingredients:

- Ribeye steak
- Pit Boss Chophouse Steak Rub

Directions:

1. Set the Pit Boss Grill or Smoker to 225°F.

2. Place ribeye in an aluminum pan and sprinkle the Pit Boss Chophouse Steak Rub over the top, coating well.
3. Place in smoker on the top grates, farthest away from the heat source. Smoke until internal temperature reaches 110°F to 120°F, or for about 45 minutes.
4. Remove the ribeye from the smoker and crank up the temperature to 400°F with the Flame Broiler plate open.
5. Once fire is visible, place the ribeye over grates and cook each side for 3 minutes to sear.
6. After searing, remove the ribeye from the grill and let rest for 5 to 10 minutes.
7. Enjoy!

Nutritional Value (Amount per Serving):

Calories: 480; Fat: 30.56; Carb: 2.18; Protein: 47.42

Flame-Broiled Tomahawk Steak

Prep Time: 5 Minutes   Cook Time: 25 Minutes   Serves: 2

Ingredients:

- 1 KC Cattle Company Tomahawk Steak
- 1/4 cup balsamic vinegar
- 1 1/2 tsp salt
- 1/4 cup chipotle puree
- 1/2 cup water
- Zest of one lime
- 1 garlic clove, micro grated
- 4 broken basil leaves "for garnish"
- 6 cherry tomatoes cut in half "for garnish"

Directions:

1. Preheat your Pit Boss Grill to 350°F. Once your grill reaches temperature, open the sear plate and turn the temperature up to high.
2. When flames appear through the open sear plate, start to broil the steak on all sides.
3. Once your steak is seared on all sides, close the sear plate, and set your grill to 250°F.
4. Next, place the steak on the top rack and smoke until you reach an internal temperature of 128-132°F.
5. When your steak reaches the desired internal temperature, remove from the smoker and allow to rest for 5 to 10 mins before carving.
6. Garnish with Balsamic reduction (vinegar, salt, chipotle puree, water, lime

zest, garlic), broken basil, and cherry tomatoes before serving.

Nutritional Value (Amount per Serving):

Calories: 310; Fat: 16.51; Carb: 14.55; Protein: 24.34

Garlic Butter Steak Bites

Prep Time: 5 Minutes   Cook Time: 10 Minutes   Serves: 1

Ingredients:

- B1 NY Strip Steak Or Rib Eye, trimmed and cut into 1-inch cubes
- Pit Boss Smoked Salt & Pepper Rub
- 4 tbsp unsalted butter
- 1 tbsp minced garlic
- 2-3 tbsp Parmesan cheese, grated
- Parsley, for garnish

Directions:

1. Preheat Pit Boss grill to 350°F.
2. Season steak cubes with Pit Boss Smoked Salt & Pepper Rub.
3. Heat oil and once it's sizzling, place the steak cubes on the griddle in a single layer.
4. Cook about 3-4 minutes per side for medium rare making sure a nice brown crust forms.
5. Meanwhile, in a small saucepan, add butter, garlic, and Parmesan cheese. Place on the griddle and cook until the butter and cheese has melted.
6. Place steak bites in a bowl and pour the garlic butter sauce. Toss to combine.
7. Plate and garnish with parsley. Use leftover garlic butter for dipping.

Nutritional Value (Amount per Serving):

Calories: 1621; Fat: 130.77; Carb: 7.46; Protein: 106.29

Green Chili Shredded Beef Sliders

Prep Time: 20 Minutes   Cook Time: 6 Hours   Serves: 8

Ingredients:

- 1 can beef broth
- 1 package slider buns
- Cheddar cheese, slices
- 5-6 lbs beef chuck roast, trimmed
- 1 can green Chili, diced
- 7 oz jar salsa verde
- 2 tbsp Pit Boss Sweet Heat Rub

Directions:

1. Fire up your Pit Boss Grill and set the temperature to 300°F. If you're using

a gas or charcoal grill, set the temperature to medium heat.

2. Remove the beef chuck roast from its packaging, drain any excess fluid, and pat it dry with paper towels.
3. Place the chuck roast in a disposable aluminum pan. Pour the salsa verde, diced green chili, Pit Boss Sweet Heat Rub, and beef broth over the top of the roast.
4. Place a temperature probe into the thickest part of the chuck roast and tightly wrap the top of the pan in aluminum foil to seal it.
5. Grill for 5-6 hours, or until the beef is at an internal temperature of 202°F and is tender and falling apart.
6. Remove the chuck roast from the grill and allow it to rest for 30 minutes.
7. Once the chuck roast has finished resting, use the Pit Boss Meat Claws to shred the beef, discarding any fatty parts.
8. Top the slider buns with a slice of Cheddar cheese and a spoonful of the Green Chile Shredded Beef, and serve immediately.

Nutritional Value (Amount per Serving):

Calories: 734; Fat: 35.24; Carb: 19.69; Protein: 85.5

Smoked Leg of Lamb with Curry and Garlic Marinade

Prep Time: 2 Hours 40 Minutes   Cook Time: 2.5-3 Hours   Serves: 8

Ingredients:

- 1-3, 4-pound boneless leg of lamb
- 8 cloves garlic, minced
- 1 tbsp coriander, coarsely ground
- 1-1/2 tbsp curry powder
- 2 tbsp ginger, finely chopped
- 1/4 cup olive oil
- 3 tbsp honey
- 1/2 cup cilantro, shopped
- Pit Boss GSP Rub

Directions:

1. Sprinkle Pit Boss GSP Rub over the minced garlic, and mash it with the flat side of a knife to make a paste.
2. In a small bowl, mix the garlic paste, the spices, ginger, olive oil, and honey, until the mixture resembles a somewhat thin soup.
3. Trim excess fat off of the leg of lamb. Place the lamb in a 1-gallon Ziploc plastic bag. Pour the mixture in the bag over the lamb. Make sure the lamb is well coated. Place in fridge to let marinate for 2 hours, or up to 24 hours in the refrigerator.
4. Set your Pit Boss Grill or Smoker to 250°F and smoke until it hits between 135°F to 140°F for medium rare, or around 2 1/2 to 3 hours.
5. When it's done, take it out and let it rest for 10 to 15 minutes loosely covered with foil.

6. Slice, top with some cilantro, and serve! Pairs well with roasted potatoes and asparagus.

Nutritional Value (Amount per Serving):

Calories: 257; Fat: 13.28; Carb: 10.36; Protein: 23.65

Rosemary Citrus Grilled Lamb Chops

Prep Time: 60 Minutes   Cook Time: 15-20 Minutes   Serves: 4

Ingredients:

- 2 tbsp Chophouse steak rub
- 2 pounds thick cut rib chops or lamb loin
- Juice from 1/2 lime
- 3 tbsp orange juice
- 4 garlic cloves, minced
- Juice from 1/2 lemon
- 1/4 cup olive oil
- 1/4 cup Red wine vinegar

Directions:

1. In a mixing bowl, whisk together all the ingredients and 2 Tbsp Pit Boss Chophouse Steak Rub. Place the lamb chops in a glass baking pan and pour the marinade over the top. Flip the chops over a few times to make sure that they are completely coated.
2. Cover the glass pan in aluminum foil and allow the lamb chops to marinade for 4-12 hours. Once the meat has finished marinating, drain off the excess marinade and discard.
3. Preheat your Pit Boss and set the temperature to 400°F. If you're using a gas or charcoal grill, set it up for medium high heat. Grill the chops for 5-7 minutes per side, then lower the temperature to 350°F or medium heat, and flip and grill for another 5-7 minutes.
4. Remove the lamb chops from the grill, cover in foil, and allow to rest for 5 minutes before serving.

Nutritional Value (Amount per Serving):

Calories: 754; Fat: 50.5; Carb: 3.26; Protein: 70.28

Chapter 3: Pork, Chicken and Turkey

Alabama Prok Rind Nachos

Prep Time: 15 Minutes   Cook Time: 40 Minutes   Serves: 5

Ingredients:

- 2 bags pork rinds – flavor of choice
- 1 15oz can nacho cheese
- 1/2 cup milk
- 1 diced tomato
- 1 diced avocado
- 1 sliced jalapeno
- 4 slices cooked bacon, chopped
- 1/4 cup Alabama White sauce
- 2 green onions, thinly sliced
- 1 cup shredded smoked white cheddar cheese

Directions:

1. Preheat your Pit Boss Grill to 225°F
2. Place the pork rinds on a cookie sheet and top with the cheddar cheese
3. Add milk and nacho cheese to a small oven safe pot and place it inside the grill. Close the grill lid, and allow the cheese to melt and get hot, stirring occasionally. This should take about 30 minutes.
4. Place the pork rinds inside your Pit Boss grill for 10 minutes, or until the cheese is melted.
5. Remove both the pork rinds and the cheese sauce from grill and set aside.
6. Top the nachos with the hot cheese sauce and remaining toppings and enjoy!

Nutritional Value (Amount per Serving):

Calories: 1236; Fat: 82.91; Carb: 29.72; Protein: 89.91

Apple Bacon Smoked Ham with Glazed Carrots

Prep Time: 25 Minutes   Cook Time: 2 Hours   Serves: 12

Ingredients:

- 1 1/2 cup apple cider
- 3 tbsp apple cider vinegar and 2 Apples
- 1 lb. bacon
- 2 tbsp butter, unsalted
- 2 tbsp corn starch
- 3 tbsp Dijon mustard
- Pit Boss Homestyle Pork Rub
- 1/2 cup pure maple syrup
- 1 large bone- in spiral cut smoked ham
- 2 tbsp yellow mustard

Directions:

1. Turn your grill to smoke mode, let the fire catch and then set to 250°F.
2. Smoke the bacon directly on the grates for 25 minutes, flipping at the 15-minute mark. Thinly slice the apples while the bacon cooks. Once the bacon is done, set your temperature down to 225°F.

3. Put the spiral-sliced ham into an aluminum foil roasting pan. Start by adding apple into the first slice and every other slice after that. Fill in all other slices with the bacon strips. Season with Pit Boss Homestyle Pork Rub. Add any extra apple cider to the bottom of the pan for added flavor.
4. Place ham in the grill for 60 minutes.
5. Meanwhile, in a saucepan, whisk together apple cider, maple syrup, apple cider vinegar, Dijon mustard, yellow mustard, corn starch and Pit Boss Homestyle Pork Rub. Bring to a boil. Reduce to a simmer, stirring often, until the sauce has thickened and reduced. Stir in the butter until it has completely melted. Glaze should thicken more as it stands.
6. After 60 minutes, add carrots into the roasting pan and glaze the entire ham. Glaze again every 30 minutes until done.
7. Remove ham from grill and allow to rest covered with foil for 20 minutes before serving.
8. Serve with remaining warmed up sauce if desired.

Nutritional Value (Amount per Serving):

Calories: 239; Fat: 15.13; Carb: 17.16; Protein: 11.48

Al Pastor Chicken Wings

Prep Time: 5 Minutes   Cook Time: 15-25 Minutes   Serves: 2

Ingredients:

- 3 oz. Achiote paste
- 4 oz. pineapple juice
- 2 tbsp. apple cider vinegar
- 2 tsp. salt
- 1/4 tsp. cumin
- 2 tsp. dried oregano
- 1/2 cup canola / vegetable oil
- 8 whole chicken wings or 16 wing sections
- Optional garnishes: grilled pineapple, pickled onion, and parsley

Directions:

1. Add the Achiote paste, pineapple juice, vinegar, salt, cumin, oregano, and oil to a blender, and blend until smooth to create your marinade.
2. In a large bowl, coat your wings with the freshly blended Al Pastor Marinade. Once your wings are fully coated, cover, place in the refrigerator, and let rest for 6-24 hours.
3. Preheat your Pit Boss Grill to 300°F, and place your wings on the top rack to roast. Turn the wings every 10-12 minutes until the internal temperature reaches 170°F
4. When your wings have reached their desired internal temperature, remove them from the grill, and garnish with grilled pineapple, parsley, and pickled onion.

5. Enjoy!

Nutritional Value (Amount per Serving):

Calories: 1061; Fat: 85.3; Carb: 28.7; Protein: 47.18

BBQ Chicken Stuffed Bell Peppers

Prep Time: 20 Minutes   Cook Time: 15 Minutes   Serves: 4

Ingredients:

- 1/2 cup barbecue sauce
- 1/2 cup cheddar cheese, shredded
- 2 tbsp Pit Boss Chicken & Poultry
- Rub
- 4 bell pepper
- 2 cups leftover chicken, chopped

Directions:

1. Wash and slice the bell peppers in half, long ways. Deseed them and set aside.
2. Preheat your Pit Boss Grill to 350°F.
3. In a large bowl, mix together the cheese, chicken, Pit Boss Chicken and Poultry Rub, and barbecue sauce, then stuff inside the pepper halves.
4. Grill the peppers for 7-10 minutes or until the peppers are softened and the filling is heated through and melted. Remove from the grill and serve.

Nutritional Value (Amount per Serving):

Calories: 649; Fat: 15.02; Carb: 22.28; Protein: 100.89

Bourbon Glazed Smoked Turkey Breast

Prep Time: 10 Minutes   Cook Time: 4 Hours   Serves: 6

Ingredients:

- 1/2 cup bourbon
- 2 tbsp Pit Boss All Purpose GSP Rub
- 1/4 cup maple syrup
- 2 tbsp olive oil
- 1/2 tbsp onion powder
- 1/4 cup orange juice
- 9 lbs shady brook farms turkey breast, whole, bone-in
- 1 sweet potato, halved
- 2 tbsp tamari
- 1/2 tbsp thyme, dried
- 1 stick butter
- 1 yellow onion, halved

Directions:

1. Rinse turkey thoroughly under cold water, then blot dry with paper towels.
2. Rub turkey with olive oil, then season inside and outside of the cavity with a blend of All Purpose GSP Rub, onion powder, and dried thyme. Place in a cast-iron skillet, and prop up on either side with onion and potato. Set

aside.

3. Set your Pit Boss pellet grill on SMOKE mode and let it run with lid open for 10 minutes then preheat to 250°F. If using a gas or charcoal grill, set it up for low, indirect heat.
4. Transfer turkey to the grill and smoke for 3 to 3 ½ hours, or until an internal temperature of 165 F is reached, rotating after 1 ½ hours.
5. Meanwhile, prepare the glaze melt the butter in a small saucepan.
6. Whisk in the bourbon, maple syrup, orange juice, and soy sauce. Bring to a boil, then reduce to a simmer.
7. Simmer for 10 minutes, until sauce is slightly thickened. Set aside.
8. Baste turkey with the glaze every 20 to 30 minutes, after rotating the turkey.
9. Remove the turkey from the grill and allow it to rest for 20 minutes before slicing, and serving warm.

Nutritional Value (Amount per Serving):

Calories: 1173; Fat: 25.52; Carb: 14.49; Protein: 206.65

Cuban Stuffed Pork Lion by Wicked BBQ

Prep Time: 40 Minutes   Cook Time: 2 Hours 30 Minutes   Serves: 6

Ingredients:

- 6 slices bacon
- 6 Deli Ham slices
- 6 dill pickles, spears
- 4 lbs pork loin
- 1 red onion, sliced
- To taste, stone ground mustard
- 6 Swiss cheese slices
- Pit Boss Sweet Rib Rub
- Pit Boss GSP Rub

Directions:

1. Butterfly the pork loin and pound flat if needed.
2. Season both sides with Pit Boss GSP Rub.
3. Add mustard on one side.
4. Layer the ham, pickles, cheese, and onion over the mustard. Optional-add more mustard.
5. Roll up the loin and set aside to wrap in butcher's twine.
6. Lay 2 slices of bacon down over the twine. Lay the pork loin on top, long ways. Lay 2 more slices on the top of the loin, then one on each side. Tie the loin with butcher twine.
7. Now season all sides of the loin with Pit Boss Sweet Rib Rub.
8. Preheat your Pit Boss Grill to 250°F.
9. When grill is up to temperature, place the loin in the grill, stick in a meat probe, then close the lid. Now let it go until internal temp hits 145°F.
10. Pull of the grill and let rest for 10-15 minutes, then slice.

Nutritional Value (Amount per Serving):

Calories: 898; Fat: 52.25; Carb: 9.81; Protein: 92.63

Applewood Bacon Jalapeno Poppers

Prep Time: 20 Minutes   Cook Time: 30 Minutes   Serves: 6

Ingredients:

- 2 tsp Pit Boss Bourbon Apple Rub
- 1 pack Cheddar cheese, shredded
- 1 pack cream cheese, softened
- Cut in half lengthwise, destemmed, deveined and deseeded Jalapeno Peppers
- 8 strips smoked Applewood bacon, cut in half

Directions:

1. In a large bowl, combine cream cheese, our Limited Edition Pit Boss Bourbon Apple Rub and cheddar cheese. Mix until completely combined.
2. Using a spoon, fill the peppers with the cream cheese mixture. Wrap each pepper with a half slice of bacon and secure with a toothpick. Repeat until all jalapeno poppers are finished.
3. Preheat your Pit Boss Grill to 400°F. Place your jalapeno poppers on the grill basket and grill for 15-20 minutes, or until the bacon is cooked and crispy.

Nutritional Value (Amount per Serving):

Calories: 308; Fat: 21.79; Carb: 12.67; Protein: 16.28

Bacon Wrapped Hot Dogs

Prep Time: 2 Minutes   Cook Time: 10 Minutes   Serves: 6

Ingredients:

- 1 - 2 green bell pepper, diced
- 6-8 hot dog buns
- 6-8 bacon strips, 1 per hot dog
- 6-8 hot dogs
- 2 tbsp vegetable oil

Directions:

1. Preheat your grill to 350°F to 450°F. Before placing anything on the grill, generously oil the cooking grids, using a cloth and vegetable oil.
2. Heat your grill to medium-high heat.
3. Lay a slice of bacon on a cutting board.
4. Roll the bacon and hot dog around until the bacon covers the whole hot dog. Secure with a toothpick on each end.

5. Repeat steps 3 and 4 again, by wrapping each hot dog with one strip of bacon, and secure with a toothpick on each end.
6. Cook the bacon wrapped hot dogs on the grill. When the bacon is lightly crisp, remove from the heat. This takes about 4-6 minutes.
7. Toast the buns by turning the grill up to high. Open the flame broiler. Place bun face down on cooking grids. Toast until desired done.
8. As soon as the hot dogs are done, place them on a toasted bun, pile on the chopped green peppers, and serve.

Nutritional Value (Amount per Serving):

Calories: 134; Fat: 5.01; Carb: 24.24; Protein: 1.71

Bacon Wrapped Tenderloin

Prep Time: 20 Minutes   Cook Time: 30 Minutes   Serves: 5

Ingredients:

- 1 package bacon, thick cut
- 1/4 cup maple syrup
- 2 tbsp olive oil
- 3 tbsp Pit Boss Sweet Heat Rub
- 1 trimmed with silver skin removed pork, tenderloin

Directions:

1. Lay the strips of bacon out flat, with each strip slightly overlapping the other.
2. Sprinkle the pork tenderloin with 1 tablespoon of the Pit Boss Sweet Heat Rub and lay in the center.
3. Wrap with bacon over the tenderloin and tuck in the ends.
4. In a small bowl, mix the olive oil, maple syrup and remaining seasoning together and brush onto the wrapped tenderloin.
5. Preheat your Pit Boss Grill to 350°F.
6. When the grill is ready, place your tenderloin on the grill and cook, turning, for 15 minutes.
7. Increase the grill temperature to 400°F and grill for another 15 minutes or until the internal temperature is 145°F. Serve and enjoy!

Nutritional Value (Amount per Serving):

Calories: 592; Fat: 44.37; Carb: 11.48; Protein: 35.64

BBQ Pork Chops Bourbon Glaze

Prep Time: 15 Minutes   Cook Time: 30 Minutes   Serves: 4

Ingredients:

- 4 8-to-10-ounce bone-in pork loin chops, trimmed of excess fat
- 1/2 cup brown sugar
- 2 garlic cloves, minced
- 2 tbsp honey
- 1 cup ketchup
- 1/4 cup molasses
- 2 tbsp Worcestershire sauce
- Pit Boss Sweet Rib Rub

Directions:

1. Pace pork chops onto sheet pan lined with butcher paper. Season generously with Pit Boss Sweet Rib Rub, making sure to coat all sides of the chops. Set aside while you make the glaze.
2. In a medium sized mixing bowl, combine the ketchup, brown sugar, molasses, honey, garlic, Worcestershire, and 1 Tbsp Sweet Rib Rub. Mix well, add 1 shot of bourbon, mix again until sauce becomes smooth. Transfer sauce into an ovenproof saucepan.
3. Preheat your Pit Boss Grill and set the temperature to 375°F. If you're using a gas or charcoal grill, set it up for medium direct heat.
4. Grill the pork chops for 10-15 minutes per side. Place the saucepan on the grill and allow the sauce to come to a boil. Glaze the chops on both sides and let the glaze caramelize onto the chops.
5. Grill the pork chops until they are lightly charred and reach an internal temperature of 145°F to 165°F. Remove the pork chops from the grill and allow them to rest for 5 minutes.
6. Once the pork chops have finished resting, glaze them again if you choose to. Serve immediately.

Nutritional Value (Amount per Serving):

Calories: 750; Fat: 25.28; Carb: 71.84; Protein: 59.4

Chicken and Waffle Wings

Prep Time: 15 Minutes   Cook Time: 30 Minutes   Serves: 4

Ingredients:

- 2 lbs wings
- 1 tsp paprika
- 2 tsp brown sugar
- 1 tsp garlic powder
- 1 tsp onion powder
- 1/4 tsp Cayenne pepper
- 1/4 tsp chili powder
- Pit Boss Smoked Salt & Pepper Rub
- 1 cup Bisquick Original Baking Mix
- 1/2 cup milk
- 1 egg
- 4 strips thinly cut bacon, diced and fried
- Waffle sauce
- 1/4 cup unsalted butter
- 1/4 cup Frank's Redhot
- 1/4 cup maple syrup

Directions:

1. Preheat grill to 350°F.
2. In a bowl, mix to combine paprika, brown sugar, garlic powder, onion powder, cayenne, chili powder, salt, and pepper. Season wings.
3. Grill wings until minimum internal temp 165°F. I like mine well done at 190°F.
4. Meanwhile, prepare the sauce. In a large bowl, stir together the warm melted butter, hot sauce, and maple syrup.
5. Prepare the batter. In a medium bowl, whisk to combine the Bisquick, milk, and egg.
6. Transfer the wings to a bowl and toss with waffle sauce. Place the wings back on the grill for 5 minutes or until the sauce thickens.
7. Preheat the waffle iron to high and spray with a non-stick spray. Start with all the drumettes, then the flats, cooking them separately. Dip each wing in the batter, letting any excess drip off. The lighter the coating the better. Place the wings on the corners of the waffle iron with the ends hanging out. Press down and cook until the tops of the waffles are golden brown, 3-4 minutes. Work in batches.
8. Plate the wings and garnish with bacon and drizzle with some waffle sauce.

Nutritional Value (Amount per Serving):

Calories: 558; Fat: 32.54; Carb: 38.91; Protein: 31.02

Chicken Pesto Sliders

Prep Time: 25 Minutes   Cook Time: 15-20 Minutes   Serves: 6

Ingredients:

- 4 chicken thighs
- Pesto
- 1 tomato
- Fresh basil
- 6 mozzarella slices
- Extra virgin olive oil
- Pit Boss Chicken & Poultry Rub
- 1 pack King's Hawaiian Pretzel Slider Bun

Directions:

1. Set your Pit Boss Grill to 390°F.
2. Remove the skin from the chicken thighs and butterfly. Coat the thighs with extra virgin olive oil, season with Pit Boss Chicken & Poultry, and place on the griddle. Cook on each side until the internal temperature reaches 165°F. Remove from the griddle to cool, then shred.
3. Build the sliders, starting with the bottom half of the slider buns. Layer on the shredded chicken, pesto, mozzarella, and sliced tomatoes.
4. Close the sliders up with the top buns, slice, and enjoy!

Nutritional Value (Amount per Serving):

Calories: 797; Fat: 53.22; Carb: 21.37; Protein: 55.4

Chicken Spiedies

Prep Time: 10 Minutes   Cook Time: 20 Minutes   Serves: 5

Ingredients:

- 3 cups Italian dressing
- 1 cup mayo
- Zest and juice of 4 lemons
- 2 tbsp dried oregano
- 2 tsp black pepper
- 1 tsp granulated garlic
- 3 lbs boneless, skinless chicken thighs (large dice)
- 10 Peppadew peppers (garnish)
- 1/4 cup chopped parsley

Directions:

1. Combine dressing, mayo, lemon zest and juice, oregano, pepper, and garlic in a mixing bowl. This will be your marinade.
2. Add diced chicken to the marinade, leaving about 2 ½ cups aside for dressing the cooked spiedies, and let sit for about 1 hour.
3. Preheat your Pit Boss grill to 400°F.
4. Skewer the diced and marinated chicken and season lightly with salt.
5. Place the skewered chicken directly onto the grill grates of your pellet grill and cook for 20 minutes, or until your chicken reaches an internal temperature of 165°F.
6. Remove the chicken from the grill, dress with the marinade that was set aside, and garnish with peppadew peppers and chopped parsley.
7. Enjoy!

Nutritional Value (Amount per Serving):

Calories: 1023; Fat: 61.42; Carb: 90.8; Protein: 28.34

Garlic Sriracha Chicken Wings

Prep Time: 1 Hour   Cook Time: 2 Hours 40 Minutes   Serves: 8

Ingredients:

- 1 cup Buffalo sauce
- 2 tbsp garlic powder

- 1/2 tbsp Pit Boss Sweet Heat Rub
- 1/3 cup, divided sriracha sauce
- 6 lbs chicken wings
- 1 tsp pepper
- 1 tsp salt

Directions:

1. In a 2-gallon plastic bag, add ¼ cup Sriracha, garlic powder, Pit Boss Sweet Heat Rub, salt, and pepper. Mix to combine, then add chicken wings to bag. Seal the bag and massage to evenly coat wings. Place in refrigerator for 1 hour up to overnight. Set aside the remaining sauce for the recipe.
2. In a non-stick sauce pot, add the remaining Sriracha and buffalo sauce. Stir to combine and set aside.
3. Preheat your Pit Boss Grill to 250°F. If using a gas or charcoal grill, set it to low heat with indirect heat. Place marinated wings directly on grill grate and cook (covered) for 1 hour 15 minutes.
4. Flip wings and baste each piece with Sriracha sauce. Season with additional Pit Boss Sweet Heat Rub, cover, and continue to grill for an additional 1 hour 15 minutes.
5. Remove wings from grill and place on sheet tray. Baste with additional sauce, then open Sear Slide and return wings to the grill. Grill for 3-5 minutes, rotating often, until wings begin to char lightly.
6. Transfer wings to a serving tray, baste with remaining sauce and serve!

Nutritional Value (Amount per Serving):

Calories: 504; Fat: 12.32; Carb: 17.61; Protein: 75.72

Chapter 4: Fish and Seafood

Blackened Salmon

Prep Time: 10 Minutes   Cook Time: 15 Minutes   Serves: 4

Ingredients:

- 2 lb salmon filet, scaled and deboned
- 4 tbsp sweet rib rub
- 2 tbsp olive oil
- 2 cloves garlic, minced
- 1 tbsp Cayenne pepper (optional)

Directions:

1. Preheat your Pit Boss Grill to 350°F.
2. Remove the skin from the salmon and discard. Brush the salmon on both sides with olive oil, then rub the salmon fillet with the minced garlic, cayenne pepper and Pit Boss Sweet Rib Rub.
3. Grill the salmon for 5 minutes on one side. Flip the salmon and then grill for another 5 minutes, or until the salmon reaches an internal temperature of 145°F. Remove from the grill and serve.

Nutritional Value (Amount per Serving):

Calories: 850; Fat: 32.92; Carb: 1.54; Protein: 137.83

Baltimore Smoked Crab Dip

Prep Time: 15 Minutes   Cook Time: 1 Hour 30 Minutes   Serves: 5

Ingredients:

- 1 cup vegetable stock
- 1 yellow onion, minced
- 8 oz cream cheese
- 8 oz sour cream
- 2 tbsp fresh thyme
- 1/2 oz fresh chopped oregano
- 1/2 tsp Pit Boss Smoked Salt and

Pepper Rub
- 2 tsp. salt
- 2 tbsp butter
- 32 oz. lump crab
- 2 tbsp chopped parsley
- 2 tbsp Avocado oil
- 1 bag toasted pita bread

Directions:

1. Preheat your Pit Boss grill or smoker to 275°F and place a cast iron skillet over the open sear plate
2. Add your stock, chopped onion, cream cheese, sour cream, thyme, oregano, salt, pepper and butter to the heated skillet.
3. Cook for 1 hour, stirring every 15 minutes
4. After an hour, remove the dip from the grill and set aside.
5. In a medium-sized bowl, add crab, bacon, lemon zest, lemon juice, parsley, and avocado oil together and mix well.
6. Top the dip in the cast iron skillet with this crab mixture, and place back

on the grill for 20 minutes until heated through. You can skip this step if you'd like to serve the crab dip cold.

7. Finally, serve with toasted pita bread and enjoy!

Nutritional Value (Amount per Serving):

Calories: 884; Fat: 74.54; Carb: 38.84; Protein: 20.3

Blackened Catfish

Prep Time: 30 Minutes   Cook Time: 10 Minutes   Serves: 4

Ingredients:

- 1 cup Pit Boss Sweet Heat Rub
- 1 tsp granulated garlic
- 1 tsp onion powder
- 1 tsp pepper
- 1 tbsp smoked paprika
- ¼ tsp Cayenne pepper
- 1 tsp ground thyme
- 1 tsp ground oregano
- 4 (5-oz.) skinless catfish fillets
- 1 stick unsalted butter

Directions:

1. In a small bowl, combine the Pit Boss Sweet Heat Rub, smoked paprika, onion powder, granulated garlic, ground oregano, ground thyme, pepper and cayenne pepper.
2. Sprinkle fish with salt and let rest for 20 minutes.
3. Preheat your Pit Boss Grill to 450°F. Place Cast Iron Skillet on the grill and let it preheat.
4. While grill is preheating, sprinkle catfish fillets with seasoning mixture, pressing gently to adhere. Add half the butter to preheated cast iron skillet and swirl to coat, add more butter if needed. Place fillets in hot skillet and cook 3-5 minutes or until a dark crust has been formed. Flip and cook an additional 3-5 minutes or until the fish flakes apart when pressed gently with your finger.
5. Remove fish from grill and sprinkle evenly with fresh parsley.
6. Serve with lemon wedges and enjoy!

Nutritional Value (Amount per Serving):

Calories: 239; Fat: 12.63; Carb: 3.75; Protein: 27.35

Cedar Plank Salmon

Prep Time: 20 Minutes   Cook Time: 20 Minutes   Serves: 4

Ingredients:

- 1/4 cup brown sugar
- 1/2 tablespoon olive oil

- Pit Boss Competition Smoked Seasoning
- 4 salmon fillets, skin off

Directions:

1. Soak the untreated cedar plank in water for 24 hours before grilling. When ready to grill, remove and wipe down.
2. Start up your grill. Then, set the temperature to 350°F.
3. In a small bowl, mix the brown sugar, oil, and Lemon Pepper, Garlic, and Herb seasoning. Rub generously over the salmon fillets.
4. Place the plank over indirect heat, then lay the salmon on the plank and grill for 15-20 minutes, or until the salmon is cooked through and flakes easily with a fork. Remove from the heat and serve immediately.

Nutritional Value (Amount per Serving):

Calories: 526; Fat: 16.2; Carb: 25.83; Protein: 66.01

Cedar Plank Salmon with Dill Compound Butter

Prep Time: 20 Minutes   Cook Time: 15 Minutes   Serves: 4

Ingredients:

- 3 lb. butter diced
- Lemon zest
- 1 1/2 cups chopped dill
- 1 1/2 cups capers "rinsed"
- 1 tbsp salt
- 1 tbsp black pepper
- 4 portions of salmon (6-7 oz each)
- 2 cedar planks
- 10 oz dill compound butter

Directions:

1. Create the Compound Butter by combining the butter, lemon zest, dill, capers, salt, and pepper, and allow it to soften to room temperature.
2. Place both cedar planks in a container of water, and let soak for 10-20 mins, ensuring the planks are fully submerged.
3. Preheat your Pit Boss Grill to 325°F
4. Once the planks are done soaking, remove them from the water, and place them on the Pit Boss to preheat.
5. Section half of the compound butter, about 5 oz, and spread evenly atop the salmon portions. Use the other half of the butter to spread on the preheated cedar planks.
6. Once the cedar planks and the salmon portions have been buttered, position the salmon onto the cedar planks. Then, place the planks directly on the upper rack of your pellet grill and bake for 15 minutes, or until desired tenderness.
7. Remove from the pellet grill, and enjoy!

Nutritional Value (Amount per Serving):

Calories: 1216; Fat: 134.95; Carb: 2.19; Protein: 5.92

Grilled Lobster Tails

Prep Time: 10 Minutes   Cook Time: 10 Minutes   Serves: 2

Ingredients:

- 1 tbsp fish & sea rub
- 2 tbsp chives, chopped
- 3 (7-ounce) lobster, tail
- Lemon, sliced
- To taste, Pit Boss Smoked Salt & Pepper Rub
- 3/4 stick butter, room temperature
- 1 clove garlic, minced

Directions:

1. Start your Grill on "SMOKE" with the lid open until a fire is established in the burn pot (3-7 minutes).
2. Preheat grill to 350°F.
3. Blend butter, chives, minced garlic, and black pepper in a small bowl. Cover with plastic wrap and set aside.
4. Butterfly the tails down the middle of the softer underside of the shell. Don't cut entirely through the center of the meat. Brush the tails with olive oil and season with salt, to your liking.
5. Grill lobsters cut side down about 5 minutes until the shells are bright red in color. Flip the tails over and top with a generous tablespoon of herb butter. Grill for another 4 minutes, or until the lobster meat is an opaque white color.
6. Remove from the grill and serve with more herb butter and lemon wedges.

Nutritional Value (Amount per Serving):

Calories: 634; Fat: 48.6; Carb: 4; Protein: 43.27

Grilled Mahi Mahi Tacos

Prep Time: 15 Minutes   Cook Time: 10 Minutes   Serves: 4

Ingredients:

- 20 oz Mahi Mahi (skinned and cleaned)
- 2 tablespoons Pit Boss Chicken & Poultry Rub
- 12 corn tortillas
- 1 mango
- 1/2 red onion, small dice
- 1/2 red pepper, small dice

- 1 avocado
- 1 lime, juiced
- To taste salt and pepper
- 4 tbsp cilantro, chopped

Directions:

1. Preheat Pit Boss grill to SMOKE and let it run with lid open for 10 minutes then preheat to 400°F and open the sear slide.
2. Peel the mango and cut away the meat from the seed. Chop the mango into a medium dice. Do the same with the avocado.
3. In a medium sized bowl, combine the mango and avocado with the diced red onion, chopped cilantro and red pepper.
4. Season the salsa with the juice of 1 lime and salt and pepper.
5. Season the Mahi Mahi with Pit Boss Chicken & Poultry Rub.
6. Grill the fish for 6-10 minutes turning and flipping as needed. Cook until the fish reached an internal temperature of 155°F.
7. Place the corn tortilla on the grill for 15-20 seconds each side, just enough to toast.
8. Build the tacos with a portion of the cooked Mahi Mahi, topped with the mango avocado salsa.
9. Garnish with additional chopped cilantro.

Nutritional Value (Amount per Serving):

Calories: 393; Fat: 9.95; Carb: 71.78; Protein: 10.21

Grilled Oyster Trio

Prep Time: 10 Minutes   Cook Time: 20 Minutes   Serves: 4

Ingredients:

- 12 medium/large oysters
- Softened butter
- Pit Boss Maple Chipotle Rub
- Chopped parsley
- Lime juice
- Oyster sauce
- Wasabi oil
- Toasted sesame seeds
- Thinly sliced green onion
- Creamed spinach
- Toasted breadcrumbs

Directions:

1. Shuck the oysters using an oyster knife and set aside.
2. Preheat the Pit Boss Grill to 250°F.
3. Add a teaspoon of softened butter to 4 of the oysters, creamed spinach to another 4 oysters, and leave the remaining 4 oysters plain.
4. Once your Pit Boss is preheated, place all the oysters on the top rack of your grill and grill for 15-20 minutes.
5. Remove the oysters from the grill, and garnish 3 ways:
6. Top the buttered oysters with Pit Boss Maple Chipotle Rub, lime juice, and

chopped parsley for our take on a "Traditional" oyster.

7. Top the creamed spinach oysters with toasted breadcrumbs for a classic "Rockefeller" oyster.

8. Top the remaining plain oysters with oyster sauce, wasabi oil, sesame seeds and green onions for an "Asian-Inspired" twist.

9. Enjoy!

Nutritional Value (Amount per Serving):

Calories: 476; Fat: 28.18; Carb: 48.52; Protein: 21.19

Grilled Shrimp with Cajun Dip

Prep Time: 10 Minutes   Cook Time: 15 Minutes   Serves: 4

Ingredients:

- 1 grated garlic clove, peeled
- 1 tsp lemon juice
- 1/2 cup Mayonnaise
- 2 tbsp olive oil
- Pit Boss Homestyle Pork Rub
- Scallions
- 1/2 lb shelled and deveined shrimp
- 1 cup sour cream
- 1/2 lb. shrimp, shelled and deveined
- 1 tbsp Cajun-style seasoning
- 1 clove garlic, grated
- 1 teaspoon lemon juice
- 1 tbsp hot sauce
- Garlic toast squares for dipping

Directions:

1. Preheat your Pit Boss grill to 350°F. If you're using a gas or charcoal grill, set it to medium heat.

2. In a glass mixing bowl, add mayonnaise, sour cream, Cajun seasoning, garlic, lemon juice, hot sauce, and Pit Boss Home-style Pork Rub. Whisk together until well combined.

3. In a small bowl, add shrimp, olive oil, Cajun-style seasoning and Home-style Pork Rub and toss to combine. Set aside.

4. Transfer dip mixture into cast iron ramekin or small Dutch oven and cover with foil. Place on preheated grill and cook for 10-15 minutes, or until dip begins to bubble along the edges. At the same time, place another cast iron pan on grill and add shrimp. Cook for about 3-5 minutes on each side or until shrimp are opaque.

5. Remove dip from grill and top with Cajun shrimp and scallions. Serve warm alongside garlic toast squares.

Nutritional Value (Amount per Serving):

Calories: 420; Fat: 27.76; Carb: 8.48; Protein: 32.96

Grilled Spicy Lime Shrimp

Prep Time: 30 Minutes   Cook Time: 5 Minutes   Serves: 4

Ingredients:

- 2 tbsp Pit Boss Sweet Heat Rub
- 1 large lime, juiced
- 1/2 cup olive oil

Directions:

1. In a bowl, whisk together the lime juice, olive oil, and Sweet Heat Rub.
2. Pour it into a resealable bag, add the shrimp, toss the coat, let it marinate for 30 minutes.
3. Start your Grill on "smoke" with the lid open until a fire is established in the burn pot (3-7 minutes). Preheat to 400°F.
4. Place the shrimp on skewers, place on the grill, and grill each side for about two minutes until it's done.
5. Once finished, remove the shrimp from the grill and serve.

Nutritional Value (Amount per Serving):

Calories: 242; Fat: 27.01; Carb: 1.07; Protein: 0.09

Grilled Surf and Turf

Prep Time: 30 Minutes   Cook Time: 20 Minutes   Serves: 3

Ingredients:

- 2 12-14oz rib eye steaks
- 12 medium shrimp (split lengthwise)
- 1 lb. softened butter
- 2 tbsp Sriracha
- 1/2 cup roasted garlic cloves
- 2 tsp salt
- Zest & juice of 1 lime
- Chives - for garnishing
- Cherry tomatoes - for garnishing

Directions:

1. Preheat your Pit Boss Grill to 250°F.
2. While your grill is heating up, season the steaks with salt and pepper.
3. Prepare the compound butter by combining softened butter, Sriracha, garlic, salt, and lime juice and zest in a bowl and set aside.
4. Place the seasoned steaks on the top rack of your Pit Boss, and smoke until they reach an internal temperature of 110°F.
5. Turn your grill up to the highest temperature and open the sear plate.
6. Sear steaks over the open flame until they're a crisp golden brown on both sides. Remove from the heat and allow to rest 10-15 minutes.
7. With the sear plate still open, place a cast iron skillet over the flame.
8. Sauté the shrimp until they curl up, then add your premade chili

compound butter to finish them off.

9. Slice the rested steaks and plate with sautéed shrimp.
10. Top with butter, then garnish with chive and seasoned cherry tomatoes.
11. Enjoy!

Nutritional Value (Amount per Serving):

Calories: 1304; Fat: 138.92; Carb: 9.89; Protein: 19.94

Honey-soy Glazed Salmon

Prep Time: 5 Minutes   Cook Time: 6 Minutes   Serves: 4

Ingredients:

- 2 tsp Pit Boss Alberta Black Gold Rub
- 1 tsp chili paste
- Chives, chopped
- 2 grate garlic, cloves
- 2 tbsp minced ginger, fresh
- 1 tsp honey
- 2 tbsp lemon, juice
- 4 salmon, fillets (skin removed)
- 1 tsp sesame oil
- 2 tbsp soy sauce, low sodium

Directions:

1. Preheat your Pit Boss Grill to 400°F.
2. Take the salmon and place it in a large resealable plastic bag, and then top with all remaining ingredients, except the chives. Seal the plastic bag and toss evenly to coat the salmon. Marinade in the refrigerator for 20 minutes.
3. After the salmon has been marinating for 20 minutes, place salmon on a flat pan or right on the grates and grill for about 3 minutes, and then flip and grill on the second side for about 3 minutes. Turn off the Grill, remove the pan from grill, plate, garnish with chives.

Nutritional Value (Amount per Serving):

Calories: 134; Fat: 6.78; Carb: 5.53; Protein: 12.56

Shrimp Scampi

Prep Time: 10 Minutes   Cook Time: 5 Minutes   Serves: 3

Ingredients:

- 2 tsp Pit Boss Alberta Black Gold Rub
- 1/2 tsp chili pepper flakes
- To taste, lemon wedges, for serving
- Linguine, cooked
- 1 1/2 lbs shrimp, peeled & deveined

- 1/2 cup butter, cubed, divided
- 3 garlic cloves, minced
- 1 lemon, juice & zest
- 3 tbsp parsley, chopped

Directions:

1. Preheat your Pit Boss Grill to 400°F.
2. Add half of the butter to the griddle, then sauté the garlic, Pit Boss Alberta Black Gold Rub, and chili flakes for 1 minute, until fragrant.
3. Add the shrimp, turning occasionally for 2 minutes, until opaque.
4. Add the remaining butter, parsley, lemon zest and juice. Toss the shrimp to coat in lemon butter, then remove from the griddle, and transfer to a serving bowl.
5. Serve immediately, with fresh lemon wedges, and toasted baguette. Serve over linguine, spaghetti or zucchini noodles, if desired.

Nutritional Value (Amount per Serving):

Calories: 604; Fat: 34.07; Carb: 27.37; Protein: 47.61

Shrimp Tacos with Lime Crema

Prep Time: 10 Minutes   Cook Time: 10 Minutes   Serves: 4

Ingredients:

- 1/4 head cabbage, shredded
- 2 tsp Cilantro, chopped
- 8 Corn Tortillas
- 1/2 lime, cut into wedges
- 1/4 cup Mayonnaise
- To taste, Pit Boss Alberta Black Gold Rub
- Out of stock
- 1/4 red bell pepper, chopped
- 1 lb. shrimp, peeled & deveined
- 1/4 cup sour cream
- 2 tsp. vegetable oil
- 1/2 white onion, chopped

Directions:

1. In a small mixing bowl, stir together mayonnaise, sour cream, and fresh lime juice. Season to taste with Pit Boss Alberta Black Gold Rub. Set aside.
2. Place shrimp in a medium bowl. Season with Pit Boss Alberta Black Gold Rub, then drizzle with vegetable oil. Toss by hand to coat well then set aside.
3. In a small mixing bowl, combine jalapeño, onion, red bell pepper, and cilantro. Set aside.
4. Preheat your Pit Boss Grill to 400°F.
5. Place tortillas on the griddle to warm each side, then turn off the burner below.
6. Transfer shrimp to the hot griddle, and cook for 4 to 6 minutes, tossing

occasionally, until opaque. For spicier shrimp, season with additional Alberta Black Gold Rub.

7. Assemble tacos with shredded cabbage, shrimp, pepper mixture, then drizzle with sauce. Serve warm with fresh lime wedges.

Nutritional Value (Amount per Serving):

Calories: 355; Fat: 12.96; Carb: 30.28; Protein: 29.69

Smoky Clam Chowder Dip

Prep Time: 15 Minutes   Cook Time: 2 Hours   Serves: 5

Ingredients:

- 2 10oz cans chopped clams w/ juice
- 3 celery sticks, minced
- 1/2 yellow onion, minced
- 8 oz Cream Cheese
- 8 oz sour cream
- 2 Tbsp fresh picked thyme
- 1/2 oz fresh chopped oregano
- 5 slices cooked bacon, chopped
- 1/2 tsp Pit Boss Smoked Salt and Pepper
- 2 Tsp Salt
- 1 bag unsalted potato chips, crushed

Directions:

1. Preheat your Pit Boss grill or smoker to 275°F
2. Add all of your prepared ingredients to a cast iron skillet
3. Place inside the smoker over the open sear plate
4. Smoke for 2 hours, stirring every 30 minutes
5. Remove the dip from grill and top with crushed potato chips
6. Serve with your favorite chips or crackers

Nutritional Value (Amount per Serving):

Calories: 523; Fat: 35.53; Carb: 40.3; Protein: 11.89

Shrimp Boil Nachos

Prep Time: 20 Minutes   Cook Time: 50 Minutes   Serves: 4

Ingredients:

- 3 ears of corn
- 1 package cream cheese

- 1/3 cup half and half
- 3 tbsp flour

- 1/3 cup Pit Boss Cajun Rub
- 1 link sausage
- 1/2 lb. uncooked shrimp
- Garlic
- 2 tbsp Pit Boss GSP Rub
- Juice of 1 lime
- 1/4 cup Worcestershire Sauce
- 1/4 cup hot sauce
- 2 tbsp Butter
- 4 tbsp fresh parsley
- 1 bag kettle chips

Directions:

1. Set your Pit Boss grill or smoker to 350°F.
2. Place the sausage and corn in the smoker. Cook sausage for 35 minutes, or until the internal temperature reaches 160°F. Cook the corn until it has reached an even gold color all over.
3. The corn will finish before the sausage. When it's ready, remove it from smoker and set aside to cool down before slicing it off the cob.
4. Use the Flame Broiler™ lever to open the sear plate and place a skillet over the open flame. Add in the garlic, roasted corn, cream cheese, half and half, flour, and Pit Boss Cajun Rub. Stir until fully combined. This should take no more than 10 minutes. Remove the skillet from the smoker.
5. Place another skillet over the open flame. Add in garlic, shrimp, and a dash of Pit Boss Cajun Rub.
6. Cook the shrimp for 3 minutes before adding in the Worcestershire sauce, lime juice, and hot sauce. Cook for another minute.
7. Add the butter and parsley and stir until butter is melted. Remove the skillet from the smoker.
8. Take the sausage out of the smoker when the internal temperature reaches 160°F. Let it cool enough to slice.
9. On a large plate or platter, cover the dish with a layer of kettle chips, followed by the cheesy corn sauce, the cooked shrimp, and the slices of sausage. Enjoy!

Nutritional Value (Amount per Serving):

Calories: 719; Fat: 42.1; Carb: 68.43; Protein: 25.36

Seared Ahi Tuna Steak

Prep Time: 1 Hour   Cook Time: 4-5 Minutes   Serves: 2

Ingredients:

- 1/2 cup gluten free soy sauce
- 1 large sushi grade ahi tuna steak, patted dry
- 1/4 cup lime juice
- 2 tablespoons Rice Wine Vinegar
- 2 tablespoons sesame oil, divided

- 2 tablespoons sriracha sauce
- 4 Tbsp Pit Boss Sweet Heat Rub
- 2 cups Water

Directions:

1. Preheat your Pit Boss Grill to 400°F.
2. In the glass baking dish, pour in the water, soy sauce, lime juice, rice wine vinegar, 1 tablespoon sesame oil, sriracha sauce, and mirin. Whisk the marinade together with the whisk until everything is well combine. Place the ahi steak into the marinade and place the glass baking dish with the ahi steak in the refrigerator for 30 minutes. After 30 minutes, flip the ahi steak over so that the ahi has the chance to fully marinate on all sides, and allow to marinate for 30 more minutes.
3. After the tuna steak has finished marinating, drain off the marinade and pat the steak dry with paper towels on all sides. Pour the Pit Boss Sweet Heat Rub onto the plate and rub the remaining tablespoon of sesame oil generously on all sides of the tuna steak, and then gently place the tuna steak into the seasoning on the plate, turning on all sides to coat evenly.
4. Insert a temperature probe into the thickest part of the ahi steak and place the steak on the hottest part of the grill. Grill the ahi tuna steak for 45 seconds on each side, or just until the outside is opaque and has grill marks. Flip the steak and allow it to grill for another 45 seconds until the outside is just cooked through. The ahi tuna steak's internal temperature should be just at 115°F.
5. Remove the steak from the grill once it reaches 115°F, and immediately slice and serve. The inside of the steak should still be cool and ruby pink.

Nutritional Value (Amount per Serving):

Calories: 346; Fat: 20.96; Carb: 8.05; Protein: 31.26

Chapter 5: Vegetable and Vegetarian

Au Gratin Potatoes

Prep Time: 30 Minutes   Cook Time: 1 Hour 30 Minutes   Serves: 8

Ingredients:

- 5 lb. Yukon potatoes
- 3 cups heavy cream
- 1 cup whole milk
- 2 tbsp salt
- 1 tsp garlic powder
- 1 tsp onion powder
- 1 tsp pepper
- 3 cups shredded parmesan cheese
- 1 cup shredded parmesan cheese, for topping

Directions:

1. Preheat your Pit Boss Grill or smoker to 275°F
2. In a mixing bowl add cream, milk, salt, garlic and onion powder, and pepper.
3. Using a mandoline, cut the potatoes into paper-thin slices and add into the cream mixture.
4. Add 3 cups of shredded parmesan cheese to potato mixture, and mix well.
5. Use nonstick spray to coat your Dutch oven or oven-safe casserole dish.
6. Evenly distribute the potato and cream mixture into your Dutch oven. Note: you want the cream to be just below the potatoes. You may not need all of the cream mixture.
7. Top mixture with 1 cup shredded parmesan cheese.
8. Cover with lid or foil and bake in the Pit Boss at 275°F for 1 hour.
9. Uncover potatoes and raise the grill temp to 325°F to brown the top.
10. Remove from grill and let rest for a half hour.
11. Enjoy with friends and family!

Nutritional Value (Amount per Serving):

Calories: 616; Fat: 31.78; Carb: 62.73; Protein: 21.97

Cheesy Layered Potatoes

Prep Time: 20 Minutes   Cook Time: 1 Hour   Serves: 4

Ingredients:

- 5 medium-size Yukon potatoes
- 2 oz Parmesan cheese, freshly grated
- 3 oz Gruyere cheese, fresh grated
- 3 cups heavy cream
- 2 garlic cloves, minced
- Fresh thyme
- Pit Boss GSP Rub

Directions:

1. Set your Pit Boss Grill or Smoker to 400°F.
2. Peel and thinly slice potatoes, about ½ inch thick.
3. In a bowl, combine the heavy cream, garlic, thyme, and Pit Boss GSP Rub,

then stir in the cheese until fully incorporated.
4. Add the potatoes to the mixture and transfer to a 12-inch cast iron skillet.
5. Place skillet in smoker and let cook for 1 hour.
6. Let rest, then enjoy!

Nutritional Value (Amount per Serving):

Calories: 828; Fat: 44.68; Carb: 88.87; Protein: 22.07

Cornn on the Cob

Prep Time: 20 Minutes   Cook Time: 5 Minutes   Serves: 6

Ingredients:

- 1/2 cup butter, melted
- 6 corns, cob
- Pit Boss Smoked Salt & Pepper Rub

Directions:

1. Preheat your Pit Boss Grill to 400°F.
2. Husk the corn and be sure to remove all the silk. Brush with melted butter and sprinkle with salt.
3. Place the corn on the grates of your grill, and rotate every 5 minutes until your desired level of golden brown is achieved. Brush with butter halfway through (or as much as you feel - the more the better).
4. Serve warm. Enjoy!

Nutritional Value (Amount per Serving):

Calories: 347; Fat: 18.06; Carb: 42.18; Protein: 6.49

Cowboy Caviar

Prep Time: 20 Minutes   Cook Time: 15 Minutes   Serves: 4

Ingredients:

- 2 avocados
- 2 ears of corn
- 1 tomato
- 1 can black beans
- 1 yellow pepper
- 1 can great northern beans
- 1 Red Onion
- 3 jalapeños
- 1 bunch cilantro
- 1 bunch chives
- 2 tbsp red wine vinaigrette
- Juice from 1 lime
- 2 tbsp Honey
- 1 tbsp Pit Boss GSP
- 1 tsp ground cumin

Directions:

1. Set your Pit Boss Grill or Smoker to 300°F with the sear grate open.

2. Coat the jalapenos, corn, and avocados with vegetable oil and season with the Pit Boss GSP Rub. Place the vegetables over the grates and roast all sides, then remove from the smoker to cool.

3. Once the vegetables have cooled to the touch, slice the corn off the cob and dice the jalapenos and avocados.

4. Roughly chop the cilantro and slice the green onions. Dice the onion, tomato, and yellow pepper.

5. Open and drain the cans of beans.

6. In a small bowl, combine the red wine vinaigrette, lime juice, honey, cumin, and Pit Boss GSP.

7. In a large bowl, combine all the vegetables and toss with the honey-lime mixture. Mix thoroughly and enjoy!

Nutritional Value (Amount per Serving):

Calories: 616; Fat: 17.19; Carb: 98.64; Protein: 26.41

Grilled Garlic Potatoes

Prep Time: 5 Minutes   Cook Time: 30 Minutes   Serves: 6

Ingredients:

- 3 tbsp butter
- 1 large onion, sliced
- 2 Tbsp Pit Boss All Purpose GSP Rub
- Red potato, baby
- 3 sliced garlic, cloves
- 1 tsp chopped parsley, leaves
- 1 cup shredded cheddar cheese

Directions:

1. Preheat your Pit Boss Grill then increase the temperature to 400°F.

2. Cut and arrange potato slices, separated by onion and butter slices, on a large piece of commercial grade aluminum foil. If commercial grade aluminum foil is unavailable, layer aluminum foil until it is strong, or use a baking sheet.

3. Top potatoes with garlic, and season with parsley, and All Purpose GSP Rub. Place potatoes on the aluminum foil.

4. Place on the preheated grill and cook for 30-40 minutes or until potatoes are tender. Serve hot.

5. An option, you can sprinkle potatoes with shredded cheddar cheese, reseal foil packets, and continue cooking 5 minutes, or until cheese is melted.

Nutritional Value (Amount per Serving):

Calories: 160; Fat: 8.12; Carb: 17.29; Protein: 5.22

Elote with Chorizo

Prep Time: 10 Minutes   Cook Time: 45 Minutes   Serves: 6

Ingredients:

- 1 lb Chorizo sausage
- 6 ears Corn on the Cob (in the husk)
- 1/2 cup Mayonnaise
- 1/4 cup Sweet Heat Rub
- 1/4 cup Cilantro, Chopped
- 1 cup Cotija Cheese, shredded
- 1/2 cup sour cream

Directions:

1. Fire up your Pit Boss Grill to 400°F.
2. Leaving the corn in the husks, place them on the upper rack and close the lid.
3. Allow to cook for 25-35 minutes or until corn is tender.
4. While the corn is roasting, cook off the chorizo in a sauté pan.
5. Combine the sour cream and mayo. Season with Sweet Heat Rub.
6. Once the corn is tender, pull back the husk.
7. Open the sear slide and mark off the corn.
8. Sprinkle with more Sweet Heat Rub if desired.
9. Spread the corn with the mayo mixture and sprinkle with cotija cheese.
10. Spread the chorizo and cilantro over top and enjoy.

Nutritional Value (Amount per Serving):

Calories: 501; Fat: 30.4; Carb: 42.12; Protein: 24.07

Gluten Free Stuffing

Prep Time: 20 Minutes   Cook Time: 1 Hour 10 Minutes   Serves: 9

Ingredients:

- 1 gluten free bread, baguette
- 4 - 5 tbsp butter
- 4 celery, stick
- 2/3 cup Craisins
- 2/3 cup crumbled feta cheese
- 1 tbsp Pit Boss Chicken & Poultry Rub
- Paprika, powder
- 1/8 cup broth, chicken
- 10 - 14 mini peeled carrot
- Cinnamon, ground
- 1 egg
- 1 White onion, sweet

Directions:

1. Preheat your grill to 350°F.
2. Tear the gluten free baguette, into crouton sized pieces, into a large mixing bowl.
3. Melt the butter on medium heat. Dice the onion, carrots and celery, and

add it to the pan with butter.

4. Sauté until the onions are translucent - about 10 minutes.

5. Add the pan mixture to the torn bread pieces. Mix. Add 1 egg to the bowl. Mix. Add 2/3 cup Craisins (we used the lower sugar variety), and 2/3 cup crumbled feta. Mix.

6. Sprinkle with cinnamon, paprika, and Pit Boss Chicken & Poultry Rub. Add 1/8 cup bone broth. Mix again.

7. Mix ingredients until evenly coated and distributed. Should be moist but not overly sticky.

8. Add ingredients into a baking dish (coat with Crisco or another shortening) and cover with tin foil. Bake on the grill for 50-55 minutes. Rotate every 15ish minutes. Remove tin foil and bake for another 10 minutes.

9. Remove the stuffing from your grill, let it cool for about 10 minutes.

Nutritional Value (Amount per Serving):

Calories: 265; Fat: 11.42; Carb: 36.51; Protein: 7.4

Grilled Stone Fruit and Beet Salad

Prep Time: 15 Minutes   Cook Time: 15 Minutes   Serves: 5

Ingredients:

- 1 cup cider vinegar
- 1/2 a shallot
- 1 garlic clove
- 1 1/2 tbsp honey
- 1 tsp salt
- 1/2 tsp Dijon mustard
- 3/4 cup Canola oil
- 4 oz goat cheese
- 1/2 tsp black pepper
- 3 peaches or stone fruit of choice cut into 6 equal pieces
- 10-12 oz baby kale or mixed green of choice
- 6 beets cut into 8 pieces from Melissa's Produce
- 1/4 cup melted butter
- 8-10 walnut halves from Melissa's Produce

Directions:

1. Add vinegar, shallot, and garlic to a small sauce pot, reduce by half, then cool to 40°F. In a blender, add the cooled reduction, honey, salt, mustard, goat cheese, and pepper. Turn the blender on medium-to-medium high speed, then slowly add oil to create an emulsion. Finally, chill dressing to 40°F before serving.

2. Preheat your Pit Boss Grill to 350-400°F
3. While your grill is preheating, toss the stone fruit in melted butter and season with salt
4. Once your grill is preheated, open the flame broiler and sear the sliced stone fruit until it's "grill marked", then remove them from the grill.
5. Place greens in a large bowl and top with the grilled stone fruit, walnuts, beets, and prepared dressing.
6. Toss and enjoy!

Nutritional Value (Amount per Serving):

Calories: 1029; Fat: 84.21; Carb: 60.24; Protein: 19.93

Grilled Sweet Potato Casserole

Prep Time: 1 Hour 30 Minutes   Cook Time: 1 Hour 30 Minutes   Serves: 4

Ingredients:

- 1/4 cup brown sugar
- Butter, softened
- 4 oz shopped pecans
- 1/2 tsp cinnamon
- 6 oz. mini Marshmallows
- 2 tsp Pit Boss Sweet Rib Rub
- 4 sweet potatoes

Directions:

1. Preheat your Pit Boss Grill to 400°F.
2. Wash and scrub potatoes then pat dry with paper towel.
3. Coat outside of potatoes generously in softened butter then set butter aside. Place the sweet potatoes directly on the grill grate and smoke until soft, 1 to 1 ½ hours depending on the size of your sweet potatoes.
4. Remove the sweet potatoes from the grill once they are tender. Coat with more butter and cover with brown sugar and Sweet Rib Rub. Slice the center of the sweet potato and press on the sides to create an opening. Stuff each sweet potato with a layer of butter, brown sugar, cinnamon, chopped pecans, and marshmallows.
5. Return to the grill and cook, covered, for five minutes, or until marshmallows are lightly browned. Remove from grill and serve warm.

Nutritional Value (Amount per Serving):

Calories: 496; Fat: 32.82; Carb: 52.72; Protein: 5.02

Grilled Zucchini

Prep Time: 10 Minutes   Cook Time: 6 Minutes   Serves: 4

Ingredients:

- 2 medium zucchinis, sliced 1/4 inch thick
- 1 tbsp extra virgin olive oil
- 1 tbsp red wine vinegar
- 1 tsp dried parsley
- 1 tsp dried basil
- 2 tbsp GSP Rub

Directions:

1. Set grill to 350°F with the sear plate open. In a large bowl, toss zucchini with oil, red wine vinegar, parsley, basil, and Pit Boss GSP Rub.
2. Once grill is hot use tongs to place zucchini on grill. Cover and cook, 2 to 3 minutes. Flip and continue cooking on high, covered, 2 to 3 more minutes.
3. When zucchini is tender, remove from heat, taste for seasoning and adjust as needed and eat right away.

Nutritional Value (Amount per Serving):

Calories: 32; Fat: 3.06; Carb: 0.57; Protein: 0.43

Holy Smoked Salsa

Prep Time: 15 Minutes   Cook Time: 2 Hours   Serves: 20

Ingredients:

- 12 roma tomatoes, halved
- 5 jalapenos (stems removed), halved
- 2 yellow onions, quartered
- 4 cloves of garlic
- 1 1/2 tsp seasoning salt
- 1 1/2 tsp sea salt
- Juice of 1/2 lime
- 1/2 bunch of cilantro

Directions:

1. Put veggies on the Pit Boss grill at 225°F for 2 hours. Wrap your garlic in foil for the majority of the time and unwrap when about 30 minutes to go.
2. Put everything in a food processor and add seasoning salt, sea salt, lime juice and cilantro
3. Mix in the food processor until it's the consistency you like.
4. Serve with your favorite tortilla chips!

Nutritional Value (Amount per Serving):

Calories: 25; Fat: 1.1; Carb: 3.56; Protein: 0.96

Lemon Garlic Green Beans

Prep Time: 10 Minutes   Cook Time: 20 Minutes   Serves: 6

Ingredients:

- 3-5 tbs butter
- 3 garlic cloves

- 1 lb green beans, whole
- 1 tsp pepper
- Pit Boss Boss Rub

Directions:

1. Turn your grill to smoke, once the fire pot catches - preheat your grill to 350° F.
2. Melt the butter in a ramekin.
3. While your grill is heating, line the grilling basket with tinfoil. Add the green beans and melted butter.
4. Add salt, pepper, and Pit Boss Rub to taste.
5. Add 2-3 cloves of minced garlic.
6. Toss all ingredients until evenly mixed.
7. Place basket on the grill and cook for 15-20 minutes. Toss the basket half way through the cook time.
8. Once your lemon garlic green beans are finished, remove them and add them to a serving dish — contents are hot! Caution as the butter may boil, splatter a bit.

Nutritional Value (Amount per Serving):

Calories: 98; Fat: 8.07; Carb: 6.47; Protein: 1.24

Loaded Portobello Mushrooms

Prep Time: 5 Minutes   Cook Time: 20 Minutes   Serves: 4

Ingredients:

- 8 bacon, strip
- 1 cup Cheddar cheese, shredded
- 3 cloves garlic, minced
- Green onion
- 4 large Portobello mushrooms

Directions:

1. Preheat your Grill to 350°F.
2. Core the mushrooms and remove the gills completely.
3. Sprinkle garlic in each mushroom, followed by bacon, 1/4 cup cheese, more bacon and lastly green onions.
4. Place on the grates of your Grill and cook for about 20 minutes.
5. Serve hot. Be careful taking the first bite - they're very juicy!

Nutritional Value (Amount per Serving):

Calories: 142; Fat: 7.76; Carb: 9.97; Protein: 9.85

Perfectly Grilled Vegetables

Prep Time: 15 Minutes   Cook Time: 30-35 Minutes   Serves: 5

Ingredients:

- Asparagus
- Carrots
- Bell peppers
- Bok Choy (optional)
- Green cabbage
- Olive oil
- Salt + pepper
- Paprika
- Pit Boss GSP Rub

Directions:

1. Preheat your Pit Boss Grill to 375°F
2. Chop all of your vegetables and place them onto foil pans, keeping the cabbage in a separate container.
3. Drizzle olive oil over the vegetables and season with salt and pepper + your Pit Boss GSP Rub. Season the cabbage with paprika.
4. Place the vegetables on the grill and close the lid.
5. Let everything cook for about 20 minutes and then pull off the carrots and asparagus. Let the bell pepper and cabbage continue cooking for about 10-15 minutes.
6. Once everything is off, let it cool and then disperse into meal prep containers and serve with your favorite protein!

Nutritional Value (Amount per Serving):

Calories: 122; Fat: 6.7; Carb: 16.15; Protein: 3.26

Smoked Elote Skewers

Prep Time: 15 Minutes   Cook Time: 35 Minutes   Serves: 5

Ingredients:

- 5 ears of corn
- 1/4 cup vegetable oil
- 2 tbsp Pit Boss GSP Rub
- 1 cup Mayo
- 1 cup Cotija Cheese
- Pit Boss Sweet Heat Rub
- 5 skewers - wood or metal
- 1 small bag of hot Cheetos (optional)

Directions:

1. Turn on your Pit Boss grill and set to 350°F.
2. While your grill is heating up, husk each ear of corn, and mix vegetable oil, and Pit Boss GSP Rub in a small bowl.
3. Then, place your husked ears of corn on the top grates of your smoker. Before you close the lid, brush your Oil/GSP Rub mixture onto the corn using a basting brush. Close the smoker lid and cook for 30-35 minutes.
4. Remove from the smoker when the corn is semi-soft, place onto a clean cutting board, and skewer each ear of corn.

5. Then, with a clean basting brush, coat the surface of the corn with mayo. The mayo will act as a binder for your toppings.
6. Once your corn is coated in mayo, place the corn into a bowl with cotija cheese, and roll the corn in the cheese until fully covered. Use a spoon to sprinkle cheese over the corn if needed.
7. This step is optional, but for an extra kick, you can also roll the corn in crushed Hot Cheetos, or top with our Sweet Heat Rub.

Nutritional Value (Amount per Serving):

Calories: 469; Fat: 34.3; Carb: 36.41; Protein: 10.11

Smoked Scalloped Potatoes

Prep Time: 30 Minutes   Cook Time: 1 Hour   Serves: 6

Ingredients:

- 1 stick of butter
- 1/2 Chedder Jack or Colby Jack Cheese, Shredded
- Medium yellow onion
- 2 tsp Pit Boss Smoked Salt & Pepper Rub
- 6-8 potatoes
- Smoked Gouda Cheese, sliced

Directions:

1. Preheat your Pit Boss Grill to 350°F.
2. Peel 6-8 potatoes and slice into 1/4 round slices, cover with water in pot and bring to boil, allow to boil for 2-3 minutes.
3. In the cast iron skillet, start to layer the potatoes and cheese. Starting by using a slotted spoon to remove potatoes from water. You will want some of the water from the boiling process to make it into the skillet, but not an excessive amount. Using a slotted spoon but not shaking the potatoes dry works perfectly.
4. Once you have a base layer of potatoes, add a layer of sliced onion (approx. ½ of a medium yellow onion), salt, pepper, Pit Boss Smoked Salt & Pepper Rub, a drizzle of sweet condensed milk, half a stick of butter cut into pats, and a layer of sliced smoked gouda cheese.
5. Repeat on the 2nd layer. Top with grated cheddar jack or Colby jack cheese.
6. Cook at 325°F to 350°F for approx. 1 hour or until the potatoes are tender.
7. For crustier cheese on top, turn the grill up to 425°F for the last 10 to 15 minutes or until the cheese is golden brown.

Nutritional Value (Amount per Serving):

Calories: 448; Fat: 10.07; Carb: 76.46; Protein: 14.53

Chapter 6: Pizza and Burger

Pit Boss Smoker Pizza

Prep Time: 30 Minutes   Cook Time: 20 Minutes   Serves: 2

Ingredients:

- Pizza dough
- 1 cup tomato sauce
- 2 cups Mozzarella cheese
- Toppings of your choice
- Olive oil for brushing
- Cornmeal for dusting
- Pit Boss Wood Pellets

Directions:

1. Preheat your Pit Boss Grill to 400°F and set it to the smoke setting.
2. Prepare your pizza dough and roll it out on a floured surface until it's about 1/4-inch thick.
3. Lightly dust a pizza stone with cornmeal.
4. Place your rolled dough on the prepared stone.
5. Brush the entire surface of the dough lightly with olive oil.
6. Spread a thin layer of tomato sauce over the dough.
7. Sprinkle the shredded mozzarella cheese evenly over the sauce.
8. Top the cheese with your chosen toppings.
9. Transfer the pizza stone to the grill. Close the lid and let it cook for about 15-20 minutes.
10. Remove the pizza from the grill, let it cool before slicing and serving.

Nutritional Value (Amount per Serving):

Calories: 1265; Fat: 41.01; Carb: 143.15; Protein: 77.15

Pit Boss Burgers

Prep Time: 10 Minutes   Cook Time: 12-16 Minutes   Serves: 4

Ingredients:

- 2 lbs ground chuck
- 3 cloves garlic minced
- 1 piece onion chopped
- Coarse salt and ground black
- pepper to taste
- 4 pieces burger buns
- 3 tbsp butter melted

Directions:

1. Preheat Pit Boss Grill to 400°F.
2. In a bowl, combine ground beef, onion, and garlic.
3. Make 4 patties roughly about 1 inch thick.
4. Generously season burger patties with coarse salt and ground black pepper.
5. Before adding the patties to the grates, quickly brush the grates with oil.

Now add the burger patties on the grill and cook them about 6-8 minutes on each side. Internal meat temperature should be cooked to at least 160°F.

6. Brush the 4 buns with butter and place on the grill to toast for a few minutes.

7. Place the burgers on the buns and add your favorite toppings. Enjoy!

Nutritional Value (Amount per Serving):

Calories: 497; Fat: 27.9; Carb: 12.11; Protein: 50.16

Barbecue Bear Burgers

Prep Time: 20 Minutes   Cook Time: 45 Minutes   Serves: 4

Ingredients:

- 1 lb. ground bear meat
- Hamburger buns
- 1/4 Cup Pit Boss Kentucky Whiskey Barrel BBQ Sauce
- 2 tbsp Pit Boss Memphis BBQ Rub
- Pit Boss Sweet Heat Rub
- 4 gouda cheese wheels

Directions:

1. Add ground bear meat, Kentucky Whiskey Barrel BBQ Sauce, Memphis BBQ Rub into large mixing bowl and combine.

2. Divide the meat mixture into 4 even parts, and shape each around the gouda cheese wheels to create patties.

3. Coat each burger patty with Pit Boss Sweet Heat Rub.

4. Set Pit Boss Grill temperature to high (400°F).

5. Open the sear plate on your Pit Boss and sear burgers until they have a dark brown color. Once the burgers are browned, close the sear plate and set grill temp to 300°F.

6. Smoke until bear burgers have internal temperature of 135°F.

Nutritional Value (Amount per Serving):

Calories: 502; Fat: 18.59; Carb: 47.25; Protein: 35.75

Barbecue Stuffed Beef Can Burgers

Prep Time: 10 Minutes   Cook Time: 1 Hour   Serves: 4

Ingredients:

- 8 bacon slices
- 1/2 lb cheddar jack, cubed

- 1 Jalapeno pepper, minced
- 1 white onion, caramelized
- 1 beer, can
- 2 1/2 lbs ground beef
- Pit Boss Sweet Rib Rub

Directions:

1. Preheat your Pit Boss Grill to 300°F.
2. Place ground beef in a mixing bowl, season with Pit Boss Sweet Rib Rub, then mix by hand.
3. Form 4, 10 ounces balls, then use a can (any 12 ounces aluminum can will work), and press the can down the center of each ball, creating a small beef bowl.
4. Press along the sides and roll to create a beef bowl, approximately 3 ½ inches tall.
5. Wrap beef with 2 pieces of bacon, then fill with cheese, caramelized onion, and minced jalapeño.
6. Set filled burgers in a large cast iron skillet, then transfer to the grill. Cook for 25 minutes in the skillet, then transfer burgers to the top rack. Increase the temperature to 325°F, and cook an additional 25 to 30 minutes, rotating halfway.
7. Remove from the grill, top with extra jalapeño, rest for 5 minutes, then serve warm.

Nutritional Value (Amount per Serving):

Calories: 1441; Fat: 96.3; Carb: 47.29; Protein: 91.66

Cheddar Stuffed Burgers

Prep Time: 15 Minutes   Cook Time: 30 Minutes   Serves: 12

Ingredients:

- 1 tbsp bold burger rub
- 3 lbs beef, ground
- Pepper
- Salt
- 3/4 cup bacon, chopped
- 1 Jalapeno, chopped
- 1/2 cup ranch dressing
- 1 1/2 cups shredded cheddar cheese

Directions:

1. Set your Pit Boss grill to 350°F.
2. In a small bowl, combine cheese, bacon, jalapeno and ranch dressing.
3. In a clean, large bowl, combine ground beef with enough salt, pepper to taste, and Pit Boss Bold Burger Rub.
4. Form meat into patties and place on a pan. A good rule of thumb is for each patty to be about the size of the palm of your hand.
5. Using a clean glass, press into each patty, leaving the imprint of the

bottom of the glass in the patty. Stuff the filling into the indent. Grill for 25 minutes or until the ground beef reaches an internal temperature of 160°F.

6. Serve hot.

Nutritional Value (Amount per Serving):

Calories: 254; Fat: 15.12; Carb: 3.54; Protein: 26.81

Classic Wood-Fired Margherita Pizza

Prep Time: 15 Minutes   Cook Time: 20 Minutes   Serves: 4

Ingredients:

- 1 pound pizza dough
- 1/2 cup tomato sauce
- 1 1/2 cups fresh mozzarella, sliced
- Fresh basil leaves
- Olive oil for drizzling

Directions:

1. Preheat your PIT BOSS Wood Pellet Grill to 500°F.
2. Roll out the pizza dough on a floured surface to your desired thickness.
3. Place the rolled-out dough on a pizza peel.
4. Spread tomato sauce evenly over the dough, leaving a small border around the edges.
5. Add slices of fresh mozzarella and scatter fresh basil leaves on top.
6. Transfer the pizza onto the preheated grill grates and cook for 15-20 minutes or until the crust is golden and cheese is melted.
7. Drizzle with olive oil before serving.

Nutritional Value (Amount per Serving):

Calories: 530; Fat: 18.52; Carb: 65.76; Protein: 24.19

Smoked Bacon and Cheddar Burger

Prep Time: 20 Minutes   Cook Time: 30 Minutes   Serves: 4

Ingredients:

- 1 1/2 pounds ground beef
- 8 slices bacon, cooked crispy
- 1 cup cheddar cheese, shredded
- 1/4 cup mayonnaise
- 4 hamburger buns

Directions:

1. Preheat your PIT BOSS Wood Pellet Grill to 450°F.
2. Divide ground beef into four equal portions and shape into burger patties.
3. Grill the burgers for about 6-8 minutes per side or until they reach your desired doneness.

4. During the last few minutes of grilling, top each burger with shredded cheddar cheese.
5. Meanwhile, spread mayonnaise on the cut sides of the burger buns.
6. Place cooked burgers on the buns, add two slices of crispy bacon to each, and assemble.

Nutritional Value (Amount per Serving):

Calories: 1225; Fat: 77.75; Carb: 47.43; Protein: 81.71

BBQ Chicken Pizza

Prep Time: 25 Minutes   Cook Time: 18 Minutes   Serves: 4

Ingredients:

- 1 pound pizza dough
- 1/2 cup BBQ sauce
- 1 1/2 cups cooked chicken, shredded
- 1 cup red onion, thinly sliced
- 1 cup bell peppers, sliced

Directions:

1. Preheat your PIT BOSS Wood Pellet Grill to 500°F.
2. Roll out the pizza dough and place it on a pizza peel.
3. Spread BBQ sauce over the dough, leaving a small border.
4. Distribute shredded chicken, sliced red onion, and bell peppers evenly.
5. Carefully transfer the pizza to the preheated grill grates and cook for 15-18 minutes.
6. Once the crust is golden and toppings are cooked, remove from the grill and let it cool slightly before slicing.

Nutritional Value (Amount per Serving):

Calories: 620; Fat: 32.26; Carb: 60.76; Protein: 21.49

Gourmet Blue Cheese Burger

Prep Time: 15 Minutes   Cook Time: 25 Minutes   Serves: 4

Ingredients:

- 1 1/2 pounds ground beef
- 4 oz blue cheese, crumbled
- 1/4 cup caramelized onions
- 1 tablespoon Dijon mustard
- 4 brioche burger buns

Directions:

1. Preheat your PIT BOSS Wood Pellet Grill to 450°F.

2. Shape ground beef into four patties.
3. Grill the burgers for 6-8 minutes per side or until cooked to your liking.
4. In the last few minutes of grilling, sprinkle blue cheese on top of each patty.
5. Spread Dijon mustard on the cut sides of the brioche buns.
6. Place the cooked burgers on the buns and top with caramelized onions.

Nutritional Value (Amount per Serving):

Calories: 638; Fat: 39.36; Carb: 9.65; Protein: 58.14

Veggie Lover's Grilled Pizza

Prep Time: 20 Minutes   Cook Time: 15 Minutes   Serves: 4

Ingredients:

- 1 pound pizza dough
- 1/2 cup tomato sauce
- 1 cup cherry tomatoes, halved
- 1 cup mushrooms, sliced
- 1 cup bell peppers, diced
- 1 cup spinach leaves

Directions:

1. Preheat your PIT BOSS Wood Pellet Grill to 500°F.
2. Roll out the pizza dough on a floured surface and transfer it to a pizza peel.
3. Spread tomato sauce evenly over the dough.
4. Arrange cherry tomatoes, mushrooms, bell peppers, and spinach on top.
5. Carefully place the pizza on the preheated grill grates and cook for 12-15 minutes or until the crust is crisp.
6. Remove from the grill and let it rest for a few minutes before slicing and serving.

Nutritional Value (Amount per Serving):

Calories: 415; Fat: 11.48; Carb: 65.98; Protein: 11.26

BBQ Pulled Pork Pizza

Prep Time: 25 Minutes   Cook Time: 18 Minutes   Serves: 4

Ingredients:

- 1 pound pizza dough
- 1/2 cup BBQ sauce
- 1 cup pulled pork, cooked
- 1 cup red onion, thinly sliced
- 1 cup mozzarella cheese, shredded
- Fresh cilantro for garnish

Directions:

1. Preheat your PIT BOSS Wood Pellet Grill to 500°F.
2. Roll out the pizza dough and place it on a pizza peel.

3. Spread BBQ sauce over the dough, leaving a small border.
4. Distribute pulled pork and sliced red onion evenly.
5. Top with mozzarella cheese and grill for 15-18 minutes.
6. Garnish with fresh cilantro before serving.

Nutritional Value (Amount per Serving):

Calories: 520; Fat: 17.02; Carb: 61.09; Protein: 30.37

Buffalo Chicken Grilled Pizza

Prep Time: 20 Minutes   Cook Time: 15 Minutes   Serves: 4

Ingredients:

- 1 pound pizza dough
- 1/2 cup buffalo sauce
- 1 cup cooked chicken, shredded
- 1/2 cup blue cheese, crumbled
- 1/2 cup celery, thinly sliced
- Ranch dressing for drizzling

Directions:

1. Preheat your PIT BOSS Wood Pellet Grill to 500°F.
2. Roll out the pizza dough on a floured surface and transfer it to a pizza peel.
3. Mix buffalo sauce with shredded chicken and spread evenly over the dough.
4. Sprinkle blue cheese and sliced celery on top.
5. Grill for 12-15 minutes or until the crust is crispy.
6. Drizzle with ranch dressing before serving.

Nutritional Value (Amount per Serving):

Calories: 652; Fat: 30.97; Carb: 73.27; Protein: 19.69

Pesto and Sun-Dried Tomato Grilled Pizza

Prep Time: 15 Minutes   Cook Time: 18 Minutes   Serves: 4

Ingredients:

- 1 pound pizza dough
- 1/2 cup pesto sauce
- 1 cup sun-dried tomatoes, chopped
- 1 cup fresh mozzarella, sliced
- Fresh basil for garnish

Directions:

1. Preheat your PIT BOSS Wood Pellet Grill to 500°F.
2. Roll out the pizza dough and transfer it to a pizza peel.
3. Spread pesto sauce evenly over the dough.
4. Scatter sun-dried tomatoes and mozzarella on top.
5. Grill for 15-18 minutes or until the crust is golden.

6. Garnish with fresh basil before serving.

Nutritional Value (Amount per Serving):

Calories: 614; Fat: 28.78; Carb: 67.46; Protein: 24.01

Four Cheese White Pizza

Prep Time: 20 Minutes   Cook Time: 15 Minutes   Serves: 4

Ingredients:

- 1 pound pizza dough
- 1 cup ricotta cheese
- 1/2 cup Parmesan cheese, grated
- 1/2 cup fontina cheese, shredded
- 1/2 cup mozzarella cheese, shredded
- Fresh thyme for garnish

Directions:

1. Preheat your PIT BOSS Wood Pellet Grill to 500°F.
2. Roll out the pizza dough on a floured surface and transfer it to a pizza peel.
3. Spread ricotta cheese evenly over the dough.
4. Sprinkle Parmesan, fontina, and mozzarella on top.
5. Grill for 12-15 minutes or until the crust is crispy.
6. Garnish with fresh thyme before serving.

Nutritional Value (Amount per Serving):

Calories: 624; Fat: 28.1; Carb: 63.63; Protein: 29.53

Spicy Jalapeño Jack Burger

Prep Time: 15 Minutes   Cook Time: 25 Minutes   Serves: 4

Ingredients:

- 1 1/2 pounds ground beef
- 1 cup pepper jack cheese, sliced
- 1/2 cup pickled jalapeños
- 1/4 cup spicy mayo
- 4 burger buns

Directions:

1. Preheat your PIT BOSS Wood Pellet Grill to 450°F.
2. Shape ground beef into four patties.
3. Grill the burgers for 6-8 minutes per side or until cooked to your liking.
4. During the last few minutes, top each patty with pepper jack cheese.
5. Spread spicy mayo on the cut sides of the burger buns.
6. Place the cooked burgers on the buns and add pickled jalapeños.

Nutritional Value (Amount per Serving):

Calories: 841; Fat: 46.93; Carb: 36.68; Protein: 64.4

Caprese Stuffed Burger

Prep Time: 20 Minutes   Cook Time: 20 Minutes   Serves: 4

Ingredients:

- 1 1/2 pounds ground beef
- 1 cup fresh mozzarella, diced
- 1 cup cherry tomatoes, halved
- Fresh basil leaves
- Balsamic glaze for drizzling
- 4 burger buns

Directions:

1. Preheat your PIT BOSS Wood Pellet Grill to 450°F.
2. Divide ground beef into eight equal portions and shape into thin patties.
3. Place a spoonful of diced mozzarella and a couple of cherry tomato halves on four patties.
4. Top with another patty and seal the edges, creating stuffed burgers.
5. Grill for 8-10 minutes per side or until cooked to your liking.
6. During the last few minutes, add fresh basil leaves on top.
7. Drizzle with balsamic glaze and serve on burger buns.

Nutritional Value (Amount per Serving):

Calories: 741; Fat: 36.8; Carb: 33.86; Protein: 65.32

Teriyaki Pineapple Turkey Burger

Prep Time: 15 Minutes   Cook Time: 20 Minutes   Serves: 4

Ingredients:

- 1 1/2 pounds ground turkey
- 1/2 cup teriyaki sauce
- 1 cup pineapple rings
- 1/2 cup red onion, thinly sliced
- 4 whole wheat burger buns

Directions:

1. Preheat your PIT BOSS Wood Pellet Grill to 450°F.
2. Shape ground turkey into four patties.
3. Brush each patty with teriyaki sauce before placing on the grill.
4. Grill for 8-10 minutes per side or until fully cooked.
5. In the last few minutes, grill pineapple rings until they have grill marks.
6. Place burgers on whole wheat buns, top with grilled pineapple and sliced red onion.

Nutritional Value (Amount per Serving):

Calories: 413; Fat: 15.28; Carb: 30.43; Protein: 40.02

Southwest Black Bean Burger

Prep Time: 20 Minutes   Cook Time: 15-20 Minutes   Serves: 4

Ingredients:

- 2 cans black beans, drained and rinsed
- 1 cup breadcrumbs
- 1/2 cup corn kernels
- 1/2 cup red bell pepper, finely chopped
- 1 teaspoon cumin
- Avocado slices for topping
- 4 whole grain burger buns

Directions:

1. Preheat your PIT BOSS Wood Pellet Grill to 400°F.
2. In a bowl, mash black beans and mix with breadcrumbs, corn, red bell pepper, and cumin.
3. Form the mixture into four patties.
4. Grill the black bean burgers for 6-8 minutes per side or until heated through.
5. Toast the whole grain buns on the grill.
6. Top the burgers with avocado slices and serve.

Nutritional Value (Amount per Serving):

Calories: 442; Fat: 9.81; Carb: 75.83; Protein: 19.22

Blue Ribbon Bacon Burger

Prep Time: 20 Minutes   Cook Time: 25 Minutes   Serves: 4

Ingredients:

- 1 1/2 pounds ground beef
- 8 slices bacon, cooked crispy
- 1/2 cup blue cheese dressing
- 1 cup lettuce, shredded
- 4 pretzel burger buns

Directions:

1. Preheat your PIT BOSS Wood Pellet Grill to 450°F.
2. Shape ground beef into four patties.
3. Grill the burgers for 6-8 minutes per side or until cooked to your liking.
4. During the last few minutes, top each patty with a slice of blue cheese.
5. Spread blue cheese dressing on the cut sides of the pretzel buns.
6. Place the cooked burgers on the buns, add crispy bacon, and top with shredded lettuce.

Nutritional Value (Amount per Serving):

Calories: 1182; Fat: 67.17; Carb: 82; Protein: 59.5

Chapter 7: Appetizers and Snacks

Cheesy Jalapeno Bacon Bites

Prep Time: 20 Minutes   Cook Time: 45 Minutes   Serves: 5

Ingredients:

- 15 strips of bacon
- Smoked sausage
- Sharp cheddar cheese chunks
- 2 Jalapenos
- Pit Boss Sweet Heat Rub
- Pit Boss Kentucky Whiskey Barrel BBQ Sauce (For Dipping)

Directions:

1. Preheat your Pit Boss Grill to 300°F
2. While your grill is preheating, cut your cheese into 1-inch by 1-inch squares.
3. Slice the jalapenos into 1/4-inch round slices, slice the sausage into 1/4-inch round slices, and cut each strip of bacon in half.
4. Once everything is prepped, place the bacon strips down two at a time in a cross pattern.
5. Lay down a piece of sausage, a chunk of cheese, and a sliced jalapeno onto the crossed bacon strips. Fold the bacon over the layered ingredients, and secure with a toothpick.
6. Season with Pit Boss Sweet Heat Rub on all sides before placing them directly on the grates of your preheated smoker.
7. Smoke for about 20 minutes, then transfer "these" to an oven-save container, and smoke for another 25 minutes.
8. After a total cooking time of 45 minutes, remove "these" from your smoker and let cool.
9. Serve with a side of BBQ Sauce and enjoy!

Nutritional Value (Amount per Serving):

Calories: 223; Fat: 17.13; Carb: 7.4; Protein: 11.58

Bacon Wrapped Asparagus

Prep Time: 10 Minutes   Cook Time: 30 Minutes   Serves: 4

Ingredients:

- 1 bunch asparagus
- 1 package bacon

Directions:

1. Set your Pit Boss Grill to 400°F.

2. Lay one piece of bacon on a clean surface.
3. Starting from the bottom, roll the bacon around one piece of asparagus. Repeat for all pieces of bacon.
4. Place bacon wrapped asparagus on your grill for about 25 minutes, or until the bacon is cooked. Rotate the asparagus so that the bacon cooks evenly.
5. Serve hot.

Nutritional Value (Amount per Serving):

Calories: 464; Fat: 43.85; Carb: 2.87; Protein: 15.07

BBQ Brisket Queso

Prep Time: 15 Minutes   Cook Time: 15 Minutes   Serves: 6

Ingredients:

- 1/2 cup barbecue sauce
- 2 tbsp butter
- 1 cup green chili, chopped
- Serving pickled jalapeno
- 1 cup tomato, diced
- 1/2 of one finely diced white onions
- 1 cup brisket, pulled
- 1 pound American or Velveeta cheese, cubed
- 1 cup heavy cream
- Serving salsa
- Serving tortilla chip
- 2 Tbsp Pit Boss Sweet Rib Rub
- Pit Boss Competition Smoked Seasoning

Directions:

1. Preheat your Pit Boss Grill to 300°F.
2. Let the grilling skillet heat up on the grill. Then, add the 2 tablespoons of butter and finely diced onion and sauté the onions until they are soft and translucent.
3. Next, pour in the heavy cream and bring it to a simmer. Once the cream is simmering, add the cubed cheese, diced tomatoes, Pit Boss All Purpose GSP Rub, and chopped green chilis. Make sure to stir the mixture consistently until the cheese is completely melted.
4. In a separate bowl, combine the brisket with the barbecue sauce and toss until the brisket is fully covered.
5. When your queso is ready, pour it into a serving bowl and top with the brisket, salsa, and jalapenos. You can even add fresh cilantro as a garnish.
6. Serve the queso with tortilla chips while it's hot and fresh and enjoy.

Nutritional Value (Amount per Serving):

Calories: 471; Fat: 29.93; Carb: 30.19; Protein: 19.88

Buffalo Chicken Pinwheels

Prep Time: 2 Hours   Cook Time: 20 Minutes   Serves: 8

Ingredients:

- 2 tsp blue cheese, crumbled
- 1/2 cup buffalo wing sauce, divided
- 1-2, boneless and skinless chicken breast
- 1/2 cup Colby cheese, shredded
- 4 oz. cream cheese
- 4, 10in diameter flour tortillas
- 2 scallions, thinly sliced [reserve 1 tsp of green for garnish]

Directions:

1. Preheat your Pit Boss Grill to 375°F.
2. Remove chicken from refrigerator place on grill. Grill chicken for 10 min, turning once. Allow to rest 10 minutes, then shred.
3. In a food processor, add remaining buffalo wing sauce, cream cheese, Colby cheese, blue cheese, and scallions. Process on low for 20 seconds. Add shredded chicken breast to mixture and pulse about 8 times, or until mixture is fully combined.
4. Place tortillas on a flat work surface and divide filling into quarters. Spread mixture evenly over each tortilla with a rubber spatula.
5. Roll up tortillas and place seam side down on cutting board. Refrigerate for 10 minutes, then slice into ½ inch pieces. Transfer to serving platter and garnish with remaining scallions.
6. Serve with extra buffalo sauce or ranch dressing.

Nutritional Value (Amount per Serving):

Calories: 1003; Fat: 33.71; Carb: 129.06; Protein: 42.9

Sweet and Sour Chicken Drumsticks

Prep Time: 30 Minutes   Cook Time: 2-3 Hours   Serves: 4

Ingredients:

- 3 tbsp brown sugar
- 8 chicken drumsticks
- Garlic, minced
- Ginger, minced
- 2 tbsp honey
- 1 cup ketchup
- 1/2 lemon, juice
- 1/2 lime, juiced

- 2 tbsp rice wine vinegar
- 1/4 cup soy sauce
- 1 Tbsp Pit Boss Sweet Heat Rub

Directions:

1. In a mixing bowl, combine the ketchup, soy sauce, rice wine vinegar, brown sugar, honey, ginger, garlic, lemon, lime and Pit Boss Sweet Heat Rub. Reserve half of the mixture for dipping sauce and set aside. Use the remaining half and pour into a large resealable plastic bag. Add the drumsticks and seal bag. Refrigerate for at least 4-12 hours. Remove chicken from bag, discarding marinade.
2. Fire up your Pit Boss Grill and set the temperature to 225°F. Smoke the chicken over indirect heat with grill lid closed for 2 – 3 hours, turning once or twice, until the chicken reaches 180°F. During the last half hour, feel free to brush more glaze on.
3. Remove from grill, and let stand for 10 minutes. Feel free to add more sauce if desired or use it as a dipping sauce for the drumsticks.

Nutritional Value (Amount per Serving):

Calories: 587; Fat: 26.97; Carb: 36.32; Protein: 49.45

Smoky Clam Chowder Dip

Prep Time: 15 Minutes   Cook Time: 2 Hours   Serves: 5

Ingredients:

- 2 10oz cans chopped clams / juice
- 3 celery sticks, minced
- 1/2 yellow onion, minced
- 8 oz cream cheese
- 8 oz sour cream
- 2 tbsp fresh picked thyme
- 1/2 oz fresh chopped oregano
- 5 slices cooked bacon, chopped
- 1/2 tsp Pit Boss Smoked Salt and Pepper
- 2 tsp salt
- 1 bag unsalted potato chips, crushed

Directions:

1. Preheat your Pit Boss grill or smoker to 275°F.
2. Add all of your prepared ingredients to a cast iron skillet.
3. Place inside the smoker over the open sear plate.
4. Smoke for 2 hours, stirring every 30 minutes.
5. Remove the dip from grill and top with crushed potato chips.
6. Serve with your favorite chips or crackers.

Calories: 492; Fat: 34.06; Carb: 36.24; Protein: 11.46

Smoked Queso Dio with Pulled Chicken

Prep Time: 10 Minutes   Cook Time: 1 Hour 5 Minutes   Serves: 6

Ingredients:

- To taste, Ale House Beer Can Chicken Seasoning
- 1 lb chicken breasts, boneless, skinless
- 1 tbsp cilantro, chopped
- 1 tsp cumin, ground
- 2 Jalapenos, chopped
- 2 tsp olive oil
- 1 bag Tortilla chips
- 1 lb White American Cheese, cubed
- 1 cup milk

Directions:

1. Preheat your Pit Boss grill to 350°F.
2. Score the chicken, rub with olive oil, then season with Ale House Beer Can Chicken.
3. Transfer the chicken to the grill and cook for 8 to 10 minutes, turning occasionally.
4. Remove chicken from the grill, and reduce the temperature to 225°F. Allow the chicken to rest for 10 minutes, then pull apart with 2 forks. Set aside.
5. While the chicken is resting, heat a cast iron skillet on the grill. Partially open the sear slide, then to the skillet add the cubed cheese, jalapeño, milk, and cumin. Stir occasionally, for 5 minutes, until the cheese melts. Fold in the pulled chicken, then close the lid and allow the dip to smoke for 30 to 45 minutes.
6. Remove from grill and let rest for 5-10 minutes to thicken. Serve warm with fresh cilantro and tortilla chips.

Nutritional Value (Amount per Serving):

Calories: 513; Fat: 31.35; Carb: 25.81; Protein: 31.31

Smoky Mini Baby Back Ribs

Prep Time: 20 Minutes   Cook Time: 5 Hours   Serves: 6

Ingredients:

- 1 cucumber sliced 1/8 inch thick

- 6 mint leaves, sliced
- 3 basil leaves, sliced
- 1/4 cup seasoned rice vinegar or "Sushi Seasoning"
- 1/2 tsp sesame oil
- 2 sides baby back ribs split down the center
- Teriyaki glaze of your choice
- Pit Boss Honey Sriracha Rub
- Buffalo Wild Wings Asian Zing Sauce
- 1/4 lb. softened butter
- Thinly sliced green onion — for garnish
- Toasted sesame seeds — for garnish

Directions:

1. Toss sliced cucumbers with mint leaves, basil leaves, rice vinegar, and sesame oil in a bowl or plastic bag, and set aside.
2. Preheat your Pit Boss grill to 250°F
3. Remove the membrane from the back side of the ribs.
4. Next, season your ribs with a Teriyaki glaze, and Pit Boss BBQ Rub of Choice. We used Pit Boss Honey Sriracha Rub.
5. Then, place the ribs on upper rack and smoke for 2 hours.
6. Remove ribs, rub them with softened butter, and place in a foil pan with 24oz. of water or vegetable stock.
7. Cover with film and foil, then place the ribs back on the grill to cook for another 2 1/2 hours.
8. Remove from pan and glaze with Asian zing sauce and place back on grill for another 30 minutes.
9. Remove from the grill. Slice and plate, garnish with more zing sauce, green onions, toasted sesame seeds and marinated cucumbers. Enjoy!

Nutritional Value (Amount per Serving):

Calories: 1375; Fat: 102.45; Carb: 9.06; Protein: 105.57

Sizzlin`s Shotgun Shells

Prep Time: 30 Minutes   Cook Time: 25 Minutes   Serves: 4

Ingredients:

- 1 package of Johnsonville raw sausage
- 1/2 cup shredded white cheddar cheese
- 1/4 cup milk
- Bacon
- Manicotti Pasta shells
- Pit Boss Memphis BBQ Sauce

Directions:

1. Preheat you Pit Boss Grill to 350°F
2. While your grill is heating up, remove the sausage from its casing, and add it to a mixing bowl.
3. Then, mix the sausage, cheese, and milk together and spoon into a piping bag.
4. Next, fill the pasta shells with sausage mixture, ensuring the whole pasta shell is completely full. Then, wrap the stuffed pasta shell in strips of bacon, covering all sides.
5. Once your shotgun shells are wrapped in bacon, place them on the bottom grate of your Pit Boss with the sear plate closed. Rotate every 4-6 minutes until the bacon is crispy and the internal temperature reaches 165°F.
6. Finally, brush on your favorite BBQ sauce and cook for another 10 minutes.
7. Remove from the smoker and enjoy!

Nutritional Value (Amount per Serving):

Calories: 321; Fat: 19.29; Carb: 18.77; Protein: 21.71

Pig Shots

Prep Time: 30 Minutes   Cook Time: 1 Hour   Serves: 7

Ingredients:

- 8 oz cream cheese (softened)
- 1/4 cup shredded cheddar cheese
- 1/4 cup diced jalapeños
- 2 Tbs Pit Boss GSP Rub
- 1 tbsp Pit Boss Nashville Hot Rub
- Out of stock
- 12 oz Kielbasa sausage (or 1 packet)
- 20 oz thick-cut bacon

Directions:

1. Set your Pit Boss Grill or smoker to 350°F.
2. Cut the Kielbasa into 1/2 inch pieces. Cut the bacon in half (lengthways) Wrap the bacon around the Kielbasa so it forms a "shot glass." Take a toothpick and skewer at the bottom securing the bacon to the sausage.
3. Take the softened cream cheese, cheddar, diced jalapeños and Pit Boss rubs and mix together in a bowl.
4. Place the mixture into a piping bag or Ziploc bag (with corner cut off) and pipe the mixture into the pig shot until it is just below the top of the bacon. Tip: Do not overfill, because cheese will rise.
5. Place the shots in the smoker for about 45 minutes to an hour until the bacon is fully cooked and the cheese filling is puffed and golden.
6. Remove the pig shots from the smoker. Let them cool for a few minutes before removing the tooth picks.

7. Enjoy the game with friends and these amazing game day pig shots!

Nutritional Value (Amount per Serving):

Calories: 523; Fat: 44.33; Carb: 14.29; Protein: 24.31

Nashville Hot Chicken Wings

Prep Time: 1 Hour   Cook Time: 40-60 Minutes   Serves: 1

Ingredients:

- 2 Lbs. chicken wings, tip removed, drums and flat separated
- 1/4 cup Dill Pickle Juice/Brine
- 2 tbsp brown sugar
- 3 tbsp Cayenne pepper
- 1 tsp red pepper flakes
- 1 tsp garlic powder
- 1 tsp paprika
- 1 tsp chili powder
- 1 tsp Kosher salt
- 1 tsp corn starch
- 2 pieces Texas toast
- 1 tsp honey
- Pickle Slices, for serving
- Nashville hot sauce
- 1/2 cup (120 ml) oil
- Remaining dry rub ingredients

Directions:

1. Preheat Pit Boss grill or smoker to 350°F.
2. With a paper towel, pat the wings dry. Place wings in a shallow dish or resealable plastic bag. Pour pickle juice over the top and try to ensure all wings are submerged. Cover and refrigerate for 1-4 hours (longer the better flavor penetration).
3. Remove wings from refrigerator and pat dry with paper towel. Discard brine.
4. In a small bowl, combine brown sugar, cayenne, red pepper flakes, garlic powder, paprika, chili powder, and salt. Sprinkle enough of the prepared rub over the wings so that they are coated evenly. Top with cornstarch and combine. Keep remaining dry rub aside for the Nashville hot sauce.
5. Grill your wings for 40 minutes or until a minimum internal temperature of 165°F or 190°F, if you like them well done, flipping them halfway through the cooking time.
6. Meanwhile, prepare the sauce: In a small saucepan, heat oil over medium

heat. Add in the remaining dry rub, whisking until smooth. Simmer for about 2-3 minutes.

7. Transfer the wings to a bowl and toss with Nashville hot sauce until completely coated. Plate wings and drizzle with honey. Serve with Texas toast, pickles, Ranch or Blue Cheese dressing, and plenty of napkins.

Nutritional Value (Amount per Serving):

Calories: 1587; Fat: 142.3; Carb: 67.83; Protein: 27.35

Memphis Style BBQ Nachos

Prep Time: 10 Minutes   Cook Time: 2 Hours   Serves: 4

Ingredients:

- 8 oz American Cheese, shredded
- 16 oz baked beans
- 4 oz cheddar cheese, shredded
- 1 lb chicken thighs, boneless, skinless
- 1/2 cup Cole slaw
- 2 green onions, chopped
- 2 cups heavy cream
- 2 Jalapenos, chopped
- 1 onion, chopped
- 14 oz tortilla chips
- Pit Boss Sweet Rib Rub
- 1 cup Memphis Hickory & Vinegar BBQ Sauce

Directions:

1. Sprinkle Pit Boss Sweet Rib Rub on the chicken thighs — Smoke at 250°F to 275°F until internal temp reaches 165°F — Diced up in ½ inch size pieces when done.
2. Heat cream on a stove in a saucepan on low, just to simmer. Gradually add cheese stirring continuously until melted and well combined.
3. Heat the baked beans in a saucepan on medium, adding 1/2 cup of Memphis Hickory & Vinegar BBQ Sauce.
4. Place chips on large plate or in a cast iron pan.
5. Top the chips with the cheese sauce, and then the cooked chicken.
6. Next top with the baked beans, pouring evenly over top.
7. Top with coleslaw, and finish with ½ cup drizzle of Memphis Hickory & Vinegar BBQ Sauce.
8. Garnish with onions and jalapenos.

Nutritional Value (Amount per Serving):

Calories: 1257; Fat: 80.38; Carb: 90.94; Protein: 42.36

Little Smokies

Prep Time: 15 Minutes   Cook Time: 30 Minutes   Serves: 6

Ingredients:

- 8 mini Nathan's hot dogs
- 8 slices of bacon
- 2 tbsp Pit Boss Sweet Heat Rub
- 5 tbsp brown sugar

Directions:

1. Set Pit Boss grill or smoker to 300°F.
2. Cut the bacon and hot dogs in half.
3. Wrap a slice of bacon around a hot dog slice, using toothpicks to hold the bacon in place.
4. Place the wrapped mini hot dogs onto a sheet tray with wire rack.
5. Combine the brown sugar and Pit Boss seasonings in a small bowl to create a rub. Use the rub to cover the little smokies.
6. Place the little smokies in the smoker on the top rack, allowing them to cook for 30 minutes.
7. Once the little smokies are done, remove from smoker and let rest. Then, remove the toothpicks and enjoy!

Nutritional Value (Amount per Serving):

Calories: 219; Fat: 13.88; Carb: 20.28; Protein: 5.22

Jalapeno Bacon Pull-apart Bread

Prep Time: 10 Minutes   Cook Time: 30 Minutes   Serves: 4

Ingredients:

- 1 lb. can Pillsbury Flaky Layer Biscuits
- 1/4 cup soft butter
- 1 tsp Salt
- 4 strips cooked and chopped bacon
- 1 cup shredded cheddar cheese
- 1 large jalapeno, sliced

Directions:

1. Remove the Pillsbury biscuits from the can and quarter each biscuit.
2. Place the quartered biscuits in a mixing bowl with all other ingredients listed above and mix on a low setting until all ingredients are combined.
3. Spray or butter your meal prep pan, pour the dough mixture in, and gently press down. This will ensure that the dough bakes evenly.
4. Cover the pan with the provided lid, and keep it as cool as possible until you're ready to bake.
5. When you're ready to bake, preheat your Pit Boss grill to 350°F and allow to bake uncovered for 25-30 minutes.
6. When the bread is done baking, remove from the Pit Boss, then allow to cool for 10 minutes before serving.
7. Enjoy!

Nutritional Value (Amount per Serving):

Calories: 752; Fat: 43.37; Carb: 62.05; Protein: 29.05

Chapter 8: Deserts and Baked Goods

Carrot Cake

Prep Time: 25 Minutes   Cook Time: 35 Minutes   Serves: 10

Ingredients:

- 1/2 cup apple sauce, unsweetened
- 1 tsp baking soda
- 1/2 cup butter, room temperature
- 3 cups carrot, grated
- 2 (8-ounce) packages cream cheese, room temperature
- 2 cups flour, all-purpose
- 1/4 tsp nutmeg, ground
- 1/2 cup sugar
- 2 tsp baking powder
- 1 1/2 cups brown sugar
- 3/4 cup canola oil
- 1 1/2 tsp cinnamon, ground
- 4 eggs
- 1/2 tsp ginger, ground
- 1/2 tsp salt
- 3 cups sugar, icing

Directions:

1. Preheat your Pit Boss Grill to 350°F.
2. Line the bottom of 2, 9-inch cake pans with parchment paper and spray the sides with cooking spray. Set aside.
3. In a large bowl, combine flour, baking powder and soda, spices and salt.
4. In a smaller bowl, combine oil, eggs, sugars, and applesauce and whisk together. Add carrots and stir until well combined.
5. Pour the wet ingredients into the dry. Stir until combined but take care not to over mix. Pour the batter evenly between the two cake pans. Bake for about 35 minutes in your Grill, rotating the cake pans halfway between the cook. Remove once a toothpick is inserted in the middle of the cake and comes out clean.
6. While the cake is cooling, prepare the frosting. Beat the cream cheese until smooth with a hand mixer. Add the butter and icing sugar and mix until fully combined.
7. On a clean plate or cake stand, place one half of the cake and top with a good layer of cream cheese frosting. Place the second half on top and cover with the remaining frosting.
8. Icing tip try not to lift your knife while icing. Instead make long, smooth strokes. Lifting the knife often make cause crumbs to get into your icing. Top with pecans if desired.

Nutritional Value (Amount per Serving):

Calories: 718; Fat: 36.29; Carb: 92.8; Protein: 8.27

Cheesecake Skillet Brownie

Prep Time: 10 Minutes   Cook Time: 30 Minutes   Serves: 2

Ingredients:

- 1 box brownie mix
- 2 eggs
- 1 can pie filling, blueberry
- 1 tsp vanilla
- 1 package cream cheese
- 1/2 cup oil
- 1/2 cup sugar
- 1/4 cup water, warm

Directions:

1. Combine all brownie ingredients and mix.
2. In a separate bowl, combine cream cheese, sugar, egg and vanilla and mix until smooth.
3. Grease skillets and pour in brownie batter.
4. Top with cheesecake and cherry pie filling, using a knife to blend to give it that marbled look.
5. Place in your Grill at 350°F and bake for about 30 minutes.
6. Let cool for about 10 minutes and enjoy!

Nutritional Value (Amount per Serving):

Calories: 1348; Fat: 96.42; Carb: 109.45; Protein: 18.15

Chocolate Marshmallow Cookies

Prep Time: 15 Minutes   Cook Time: 20 Minutes   Serves: 12

Ingredients:

- 1/2 cup butter, room temperature
- 3/4 cup brown sugar
- 1/4 cup granulated sugar
- 2 tsp vanilla extract
- 1 egg
- 1 cup gluten-free all-purpose flour blend
- 1/2 cup cocoa powder
- 1 tsp baking soda
- 1/2 cup dark chocolate chunks, or chocolate chips
- 1/4 cup mini marshmallows
- 1 tsp smoked hickory & honey sea salt

Directions:

1. Preheat your Pit Boss Grill or Smoker to 350°F and line a baking pan with parchment paper.
2. In a bowl beat your butter, brown sugar, and white sugar in stand mixer for 1 minute. Beat until no clumps are left.
3. Toss in some vanilla extract and egg. Stir to combine.
4. Add in gluten free flour, cocoa powder, Smoked Hickory & Honey Sea Salt Rub, and baking soda. Stir until a thick and sticky dough forms.

5. Fold in dark chocolate chunks and mini marshmallows.
6. Best method to portion these cookies is to use an ice cream scoop and spray it with a little oil.
7. Bake for 10 to 12 minutes or until cookies are set in the middle.
8. Remove from smoker. Allow cookies to cool on pan for 10 minutes before carefully transferring to a cooling rack to finish cooling.

Nutritional Value (Amount per Serving):

Calories: 228; Fat: 11.2; Carb: 30.74; Protein: 3.11

Christmas Shortbread Cookies

Prep Time: 45 Minutes   Cook Time: 15 Minutes   Serves: 24

Ingredients:

- 8 oz butter
- 1 3/4 cups flour, all-purpose
- 2 cups (for mint glaze) powdered sugar
- 4 tbsp (for mint glaze) milk
- 1/4 cup corn starch
- 1/4 tsp (for mint glaze) peppermint extract
- 1 tsp vanilla extract

Directions:

1. Line two sheet pans with parchment paper.
2. Place the soft butter in a mixing bowl. Stir with a wooden spoon or spatula until nice and smooth. Add sugar and vanilla. Mix together by hand until fluffy and well blended.
3. Add flour and cornstarch. Stir until flour is incorporated. Turn out onto a lightly floured surface and press dough into a ball.
4. On a lightly floured work surface, roll out the dough to a 3/8-inch thickness. Keep the surface and rolling pin lightly dusted with flour. Cut desired shapes and place onto the baking sheets. Re-roll all the scraps until the dough has been used up.
5. Place the cutouts in the refrigerator for at least 1 hour.
6. When ready to bake, turn your Pit Boss grill to smoke mode, let the fire catch and then set to 350°F to preheat. Bake cookies for 12-14 minutes or until just beginning to turn golden at the edges. Cool completely before icing.
7. For the mint glaze, combine powdered sugar, milk and peppermint extract in a bowl. Mix until smooth. Glaze should be thick but pourable.
8. To glaze the cookies, dip the top of the cookie into the glaze. Allow extra glaze to drip back into the bowl. Quickly flip the cookie right side up. Allow

the glaze to dry for 15-30 minutes before serving.

Nutritional Value (Amount per Serving):

Calories: 142; Fat: 7.92; Carb: 16.7; Protein: 1.26

Cinnamon & Butterfinger Pull-apart Bread

Prep Time: 10 Minutes   Cook Time: 30 Minutes   Serves: 4

Ingredients:

- 1 lb. can Pillsbury flaky layer biscuits
- 1/4 cup + 2 tbsp soft butter
- 1/8 tsp ground cinnamon
- 3 tbsp brown sugar
- 2 crushed graham crackers
- 1/2 cup butter finger bits

Directions:

1. Remove the Pillsbury biscuits from the can and quarter each biscuit.
2. Place the quartered biscuits in a mixing bowl with all other ingredients listed above and mix on a low setting until all ingredients are combined.
3. Spray or butter your pan, pour the dough mixture in, and gently press down. This will ensure that the dough bakes evenly.
4. Cover the pan with the provided lid, and keep it as cool as possible until you're ready to bake.
5. When you're ready to bake, preheat your Pit Boss Grill to 350°F and allow to bake uncovered for 25-30 minutes.
6. When the bread is done baking, remove from the Pit Boss and allow to cool for 10 minutes before serving.
7. Enjoy!

Nutritional Value (Amount per Serving):

Calories: 695; Fat: 50.34; Carb: 54.96; Protein: 7.54

Strawberry Rhubarb Pie

Prep Time: 20 Minutes   Cook Time: 1 Hour   Serves: 8

Ingredients:

- 1/3 cup flour
- 1 prepared pie shell, deep
- 2 1/2 cups strawberry
- 1 tbsp lemon, zest
- 3 stalks rhubarb
- 1 cup sugar

Directions:

1. Preheat your Pit Boss grill to 400°F.
2. Slice rhubarb and strawberries into bite sized pieces. Combine sugar, flour and lemon zest with rhubarb and strawberries. Pour into prepared pie

crust. Cover with top crust.

3. Bake in Grill for 1 hour or until crust is crispy.
4. Serve hot.

Nutritional Value (Amount per Serving):

Calories: 266; Fat: 8.24; Carb: 36.57; Protein: 2.42

Smoked S`mores Cake Bars

Prep Time: 20 Minutes   Cook Time: 40-45 Minutes   Serves: 8

Ingredients:

- 2 cups graham cracker crumbs
- 7 oz marshmallow creme
- 1 1/2 cup mini marshmallows
- 1 box yellow cake mix
- 1 egg
- 2 cups chocolate chips
- 1 stick butter, melted

Directions:

1. Set your Pit Boss grill on SMOKE mode and preheat to 250°F.
2. Line a 9x13" metal pan with aluminum foil.
3. In a large bowl, use a hand mixer to combine the cake mix, egg, butter and graham cracker crumbs.
4. Reserve 2 cups, then press the remaining graham cracker mixture into the prepared pan. Sprinkle the chocolate chips over the crust, then dollop the marshmallow creme over the chocolate chips.
5. Spread into an even layer, then sprinkle with mini marshmallows. Top with reserved graham cracker mixture.
6. Place on the grill and smoke for 45 to 50 minutes. Let cool completely before cutting into bars.

Nutritional Value (Amount per Serving):

Calories: 631; Fat: 21.08; Carb: 105.31; Protein: 7.42

Smoked Pumpkin Pie

Prep Time: 10 Minutes   Cook Time: 45-60 Minutes   Serves: 8

Ingredients:

- 1 can (14 oz) pumpkin puree
- 1 can (14 oz) sweetened condensed milk
- 1 cup evaporated milk
- 2 tsp Pit Boss Pumpkin Spice Rub
- 2 eggs

- 1 oz bourbon or whiskey
- 1 pie crust

Directions:

1. Set your Pit Boss grill to SMOKE and preheat to 400°F.
2. Line the pie pan with the pie crust and gently press into the corners. Fold the edges of the crust over the top of the pie pan. Cut off any excess crust.
3. In a mixing bowl, combine the remaining ingredients, except for the eggs.
4. Once well mixed, add the eggs and whisk until just combined.
5. Pour the pie mixture into the pie pan.
6. Place on the smoker for 15 minutes.
7. Reduce the heat to 350°F and continue baking for 30-45 minutes or until the center of the pie is fully set.
8. Allow to cool on a rack for 2 hours before cutting and enjoying!

Nutritional Value (Amount per Serving):

Calories: 409; Fat: 21.04; Carb: 41.68; Protein: 15.49

S`more Camping Cones

Prep Time: 10 Minutes   Cook Time: 5 Minutes   Serves: 4

Ingredients:

- 4 sugar cones
- 1 cup mini marshmallows
- 1/2 cup chocolate chips
- 1/2 cup chopped candy of choice

Directions:

1. Fill sugar cones with a combination of marshmallows, chocolate, and candy bits.
2. Carefully roll the cone in foil and twist closed to keep the contents inside.
3. Cook on the grates of your Pit Boss grill at 400°F with the flame broiler closed, or over embers if you're cooking over an open fire. Low or indirect heat is best.
4. Remove from heat using a glove or tongs. Carefully unwrap the cone keeping it upright and enjoy an ooey-gooey delight.

Nutritional Value (Amount per Serving):

Calories: 351; Fat: 15.26; Carb: 49.35; Protein: 4.48

Macadamia Key Lime Pie

Prep Time: 15 Minutes   Cook Time: 25-30 Minutes   Serves: 6

Ingredients:

- 3 egg yolks

- 1, 14-oz. can sweetened condensed milk
- 1/2 cup freshly squeezed lime juice
- 2 1/2 tbsp unsalted butter, melted
- 5 full-sheet graham crackers
- 1/4 cup salted roasted Macadamia nuts
- 1 tbsp granulated sugar
- 2 1/2 tbsp unsalted butter, melted
- Whipped cream For topping

Directions:

1. Set your Pit Boss grill to "smoke" mode and preheat to 350°F.
2. Make the crust by using a food processor or blender to pulse the graham crackers and macadamia nuts together. Combine with sugar and melted butter and mix until combined. Press tightly into the bottom and up the sides of an 8 or 9-inch cast iron dish. Prebake the crust for 8 minutes.
3. Make the filling by whisking the sweetened condensed milk, lime juice, lime zest, and egg yolks together until well combined, or about 1 to 2 minutes. Pour into warm crust.
4. Bake the pie at 350°F for 15 to 20 minutes. Remove from the grill and allow to cool. Once the pie reaches room temperature, cover and chill for a few hours in the refrigerator. Top with whipped cream immediately before serving.

Nutritional Value (Amount per Serving):

Calories: 241; Fat: 17.42; Carb: 17.5; Protein: 5.32

Grilled Peaches

Prep Time: 5 Minutes   Cook Time: 8-10 Minutes   Serves: 6

Ingredients:

- 3 tbsp brown sugar
- 1 tbsp Pit Boss Smoked Salt & Pepper Rub
- 1/2 tbsp cinnamon, ground
- 3 full peaches, halved and pitted
- 1 tbsp butter, melted
- Ice cream, prepared

Directions:

1. Start your grill on smoke with the lid open until a fire is established in the burn pot (3-7 minutes).
2. Preheat to 400°F.
3. Combine brown sugar and cinnamon in a small bowl.
4. Brush peach halves with melted butter.

5. Once your is preheated, place the peach halves cut side down on the grates.
6. Grill for 5-7 minutes, or until grill marks begin to form.
7. Flip peaches over and sprinkled cinnamon sugar.
8. Grill until the sugar mixture begins to caramelize, another 2-3 minutes. Serve hot.

Nutritional Value (Amount per Serving):

Calories: 148; Fat: 2.45; Carb: 32.9; Protein: 2.13

Dutch Baby with Bourbon Apples

Prep Time: 30 Minutes   Cook Time: 30 Minutes   Serves: 4

Ingredients:

- 4 small cored and sliced apples
- 1/4 cup bourbon
- 1/2 cup brown sugar
- 1 stick (divided) butter, unsalted
- 2 teaspoon cinnamon, ground
- 3 eggs
- 2/3 cup flour, all-purpose
- 1/2 cup white sugar
- 3/4 cup milk

Directions:

1. Stick a cast iron or other heat proof skillet into your Pit Boss grill and preheat to 400°F.
2. In a blender or food processor, add milk, eggs, flour, cinnamon, and white sugar. Blend until smooth.
3. Once the grill has preheated, add 4 tablespoons of butter to the pan and swirl it around to coat until all butter is melted. Pour the batter into the pan and grill for 20 minutes, then reduce the temperature to 300F and grill for an additional 5-7 minutes, until the dutch baby is golden and puffy. Remove from the grill and serve immediately before the dutch baby deflates.
4. In a large saute pan, heat the remaining butter over medium heat and add the apple slices. Cook for 5 minutes until the mixture begins to thicken slightly. Add the brown sugar and bourbon and cook until saucy. Top the dutch baby with the apples and serve.

Nutritional Value (Amount per Serving):

Calories: 502; Fat: 19.87; Carb: 70.68; Protein: 11.87

Cinnamon Roll Ice Cream Cups

Prep Time: 15 Minutes   Cook Time: 1 Hour   Serves: 6

Ingredients:

- 1 pack cinnamon rolls